How to
Start and Operate
Your Own

Bed-and-Breakfast

Also by Martha Watson Murphy

The Bed & Breakfast Cookbook: Great American B&Bs
and Their Recipes from All Fifty States

Down-to-earth advice from an
award-winning B & B owner

An Owl Book
Henry Holt and Company • New York

How to
Start and Operate
Your Own
Bed-and-Breakfast

Martha Watson Murphy

Illustrations by
Amelia Rockwell Seton

Henry Holt and Company, Inc.
Publishers since 1866
115 West 18th Street
New York, New York 10011

Henry Holt® is a registered
trademark of Henry Holt and Company, Inc.

Published in Canada by Fitzhenry & Whiteside Ltd.,
195 Allstate Parkway, Markham, Ontario L3R 4T8.

Library of Congress Cataloging-in-Publication Data
Murphy, Martha W.
How to start and operate your own bed-and-breakfast : down-to-
earth advice from an award-winning B&B owner/ Martha W. Murphy;
illustrations by Amelia Rockwell Seton. — 1st ed.
p.   cm.
Includes index.
1. Bed and breakfast accommodations—Management.   2. Hotel
management.   I. Title.
TX911.3.M27M86   1994   93-37836
647.94'068—dc20   CIP

ISBN 0-8050-2903-6 (An Owl Book: pbk.)
Henry Holt books are available for special
promotions and premiums. For details contact:
Director, Special Markets.

First Edition—1994

Designed by Paula R. Szafranski

Printed in the United States of America
All first editions are printed on acid-free paper. ∞

5   7   9   10   8   6   4

The recipes on pages 104–108 are from *The Bed & Breakfast Cookbook*
by Martha W. Murphy, copyright © 1991 by Martha W. Murphy, and
reprinted by permission of Stemmer House Publishers, Inc.

to Kevin

Contents

Acknowledgments   *xiii*

Introduction   *xv*

1   So, You Want to Open a Bed~and~Breakfast?   *1*

2   The Bed~and~Breakfast House   *21*

3   The Bed~and~Breakfast Bedroom   *39*

4   The Bed~and~Breakfast Bathroom   *57*

5   Public Rooms in the Bed~and~Breakfast   *75*

6   Breakfast   *89*

7   House Rules and Safety Features   *111*

8   *Rates, Advertising, Reservations*   129

9   *The Art of Hosting*   157

10 *Staying in Business*   171

Appendix: Resources

   Bed-and-Breakfast Organizations   181
   Bed-and-Breakfast Reservation Agencies   182
   Trade Publications   182
   Guidebooks   183
   Resource Publications for the B&B Host   185
   Reservation Software   186
   Insurance Companies   186
   Mail Order Catalogues   187

Index   191

Acknowledgments

There are a few people I want to thank for inspiration and guidance in the creation of this book. First off are all the B&B guests I have had over the years. I've been fortunate that some very special people have come into my life this way, and it is they who have continually renewed my enthusiasm for this work and made it so enjoyable.

I thank Susan Urstadt, my agent, for leading me to Henry Holt & Company and, more specifically, to Elizabeth Crossman, my editor, whose encouragement, guidance, and excellent editing have been indispensable.

Final thanks go to my husband, for his long-standing friendship, support, and inexhaustible sense of humor.

Introduction

It seems everyone I meet wants to do what I do—run a bed-and-breakfast. Since it is a profession I backed into more by accident than by design, I am always struck by the intense interest—and even envy—my work seems to elicit.

I started my bed-and-breakfast somewhat reluctantly. I had left my office job as a travel agent and wanted to find a way to earn a living at home. I was making a stab at doing some work at home for a small hand-crafted jewelry company, but I still had time on my hands. Meanwhile a bed-and-breakfast host from down the street—one of the first in our town—kept stopping by with her husband to admire the restoration work we were doing on our old house. They enjoyed watching our progress and kept encouraging me to hang out a bed-and-breakfast sign. Since they were continually turning away travelers they couldn't accommodate, they promised to send the overflow to me.

Although I didn't anticipate much business (and didn't expect to find the work profitable or enjoyable), I agreed to give it a try. I secretly told myself I'd probably close the business in a year, but in the meantime could use this new venture as an excuse to hurry up with the restoration work—which I was beginning to think I'd never see the end of if I lived to be a hundred!

My scheme to speed up work in and around the house was successful, and to my surprise, so was my B&B business. I got a lot of bookings that first year from the host down the street. And I could see that there *was* some money to be made (as well as some good tax deductions), and in the process I was meeting delightful people.

From there my business grew every year, and I learned as I went. The host who got me started had some good tips for me, and I attended all the meetings and seminars I could. Each year I got better at what I did and improved my operation. Along the way I found that an overwhelming majority of my guests were telling me that it was their dream someday to have a B&B too. At parties a crowd would gather around me once word got out that I ran a B&B; you would have thought I was an astronaut!

Because of this interest, a few years ago I began teaching a seminar on B&Bs at Brown University in Providence, Rhode Island. As with my guests, I find that people from every background you can imagine want to leave their fields to start a B&B.

What's the big appeal? Americans long for home, I think, and running a B&B certainly allows one to spend a great deal of time there. Home represents an escape from the rat race, from rude, thoughtless people, and from a world that doesn't always go our way.

As travelers who frequent B&Bs see, the business can justify grooming a property to its most exquisitely beautiful potential. Those who long to spend more time in the kitchen, baking and cooking for a *reason,* or whose artistic side would be fulfilled if only there were more time to spend in the garden, see running a bed-and-breakfast as a dream come true.

Bed-and-breakfast hosts are their own bosses—a long-standing fixture in the American dream—and therefore the shapers of their own destiny. And because there is a lot of misunderstanding about the work involved, many would-be hosts see running a B&B as an almost effortless way to make money while meeting interesting people from around the world.

All of these elements are part of what drives people to try this profession. There is some truth in all of them, but you will see for yourself what the actual balance is when you are in business.

This book is meant to be a help for those wanting to try this profession and looking for a little guidance as they get started. After nine years in the business, I see that experience has been my best teacher—as it will be yours—but I am happy to share what I've learned in the hope that your success will come a bit faster and more easily.

The tips and advice given here are, for the most part, not hard-and-fast rules. They are suggestions for ways to do things that I think will work well for anyone, but you certainly shouldn't be a slave to what you read here. You *should* imprint your own style on your B&B; this uniqueness is part of what travelers are hoping to find when they choose your home over an anonymous motel room. But just as every good restaurant, while setting its own style, follows certain guidelines regarding cleanliness, quality of ingredients, cooking standards, and so on, certain basics apply to all B&Bs.

Every minute will not be a joy. There are days every season when I tell myself, "This will be the last year I do this!" But even during those times, I usually don't have to think for long about the ways other working people are spending their days to remind myself how lucky I am.

So, welcome to the world inside a bed-and-breakfast. I wish you the best as you begin your adventure and join the ranks of hosts who share the unique and delightful profession of running a bed-and-breakfast.

How to
Start and Operate
Your Own

Bed-and-Breakfast

1

So, You Want to Open
a Bed-and-Breakfast?

*A*ll saints do miracles,
but few of them can keep a hotel.
— Mark Twain

On the Outside Looking In

*P*icture yourself wearing your favorite weekend clothes, serenely drifting down the stairs of a rambling old manse, and quietly sipping a cup of coffee in your sun-drenched kitchen as you await your first guests for breakfast. The table is set, the aroma of a cinnamon coffee cake baking fills the air, and all is right with the world. As you tie on your apron, you remind yourself that instead of making a hectic dash to the car and a forty-minute commute through heavy traffic to reach your fluorescent-lit office, you are already in your "office"—now that you're running a bed-and-breakfast, that is.

Is this daydream familiar? If you are reading this, chances are you have stayed at a bed-and-breakfast and more than once found yourself thinking, "This is the life! It doesn't look like much work; maybe I could do this someday!" Your host seemed happy and relaxed—in fact, she barely appeared to be working—the surroundings were lovely, and to top it all off she was getting paid to lead this ideal life!

If your host has seemed at ease—if you've almost felt as though she were on vacation too, as you were—she's done her job well and has hidden from you the tremendous amount of work and effort that goes into running a successful B&B. Hosting is a *job*.

Now that this secret is out of the bag, don't stop reading! By no means do I want to discourage you from your dream of someday owning and running a bed-and-breakfast; after all, it is what I do for a living and I love it. I well understand why so many people see mine as a dream occupation, for in many ways it is. But I also know that many of those same people don't have a good understanding of what is involved in owning and operating a B&B, and if they did, not all would still consider it a dream lifestyle.

While running a B&B can be very rewarding, there is much more work required than meets the eye—so much more that uninformed novices can quickly find themselves feeling overwhelmed and longing for their old jobs and regular paychecks. Therefore, as with any new venture, it's best to do some research before making a big commitment.

What Is a Bed-and-Breakfast?

Let's first examine what a B&B is and is not. It is *not* a motel or hotel—with room service, bellboys, and a front desk staffed twenty-four hours a day—and not quite an inn either. A bed-and-breakfast is a private home that takes in paying overnight guests; the price of the room includes breakfast in the morning—hence the name "bed-and-breakfast." The house is also home to the owners, who reside there and act as hosts of the B&B, although one or both may be employed in other lines of work as well. That, in a nutshell, defines bed-and-breakfast, but the variations on this basic theme range widely, as you will see throughout this book.

While no one would have trouble defining or describing a hotel or motel, there is some confusion about the distinctions between bed-and-breakfasts and inns. In my opinion, a bed-and-breakfast is not an inn (although many B&Bs are now calling themselves inns or bed-and-breakfast inns). An inn is what you might call a bed-and-breakfast plus.

For instance, when I'm traveling, if I spot an inn on the side of the road around mid-afternoon, I might stop to have a cup of hot tea, check my map, make a phone call, and freshen up before hitting the road again. Or if it's a bit later and the menu looks good, dinner at the inn might be in order. If the dining room is crowded, I can pass time having an aperitif in the pub while waiting for a table.

If you are an experienced B&B traveler, you already know that these options are not offered at a bed-and-breakfast. You may have stayed at a B&B where you were invited to join the hosts for a glass of wine or sherry in the evening (indeed, this is one of the many charms of a bed-and-breakfast stay), but you certainly weren't charged for it! To me, these differences (dining rooms open to the general public, liquor licenses, pay telephones, etc.) set inns apart from B&Bs. But since so many Americans still don't know what "bed-and-breakfast" means and *do* know that "inn" means lodging, many hosts have decided to add "inn" to their bed-and-breakfast name. You too may decide to call your own establishment an inn. That is fine. Throughout this book, however, you will find the terms "bed-and-breakfast" and "B&B" used for establishments that others might refer to as "B&B inns"; whatever the name, the information is applicable to either.

A B&B also differs from a traditional inn in the number of guest bedrooms and baths. The average American B&B has from two to eight guest bedrooms with shared or private baths. An inn usually starts with at least a dozen rooms and almost always offers private baths. By necessity, an inn requires a substantial staff, not the case at most B&Bs.

A few more distinctions: An inn may or may not be occupied by the owners, while a B&B always is. At a B&B, guests are greeted and tended

to by the owners, and it is this feature that can (and should!) make the service at a bed-and-breakfast exceptional. (More about the art of hosting in chapter 9.)

B&Bs offer guests breakfast in the morning at no extra charge, not usually the case at inns (although the phenomenal popularity of American bed-and-breakfasts has caused many inns now to offer guests a free continental breakfast in the morning). Many B&Bs also offer a complimentary afternoon tea to guests—hot or iced tea with some home-baked goodies—another difference from most inns.

Don't feel limited by these definitions; they are meant to serve as basic guidelines. Whether you've got your eye on a magnificent eight-bedroom Victorian, or have set your heart on purchasing the rambling old inn on the lake which has been a run-down boarding house for the last quarter-century, or simply plan on sprucing up the two spare guest rooms in your house, the advice, tips, and details offered in this book will apply. For anyone interested in running a large or small B&B, part-time or full-time, with or without paid help, this book will provide the information you will need to decide if this is really a business you want to try, get you started, and help you be successful.

Who Are the Hosts?

Who will run the B&B you dream of owning? Will you be the host, or will you have a partner? Will that partner be your husband (or wife), or sister, or best friend? What I have found to be the norm most often is a married woman acting as host, while her husband works outside the home at another profession. (Throughout this book, I will use the term "host" to refer to anyone, male or female, in charge of running a bed-and-breakfast.) Sometimes the roles are reversed. In other cases, B&Bs are operated by both husband and wife. This is especially true if the couple is retired, or if the bed-and-breakfast location offers a year-round business and the establishment has a sizable number of guest rooms. This combination can make full-time innkeeping a reality for a younger couple as well. But there are also B&Bs operated by mother and daughter teams, sisters, single people, two couples, and just about any other combination you can think of.

If you're considering becoming an innkeeper with your spouse or best friend, and until now you've worked separately and have "never had enough time together," be forewarned: it is possible to get too much of a good thing!

The Host's Responsibilities

In any case, whether you run your B&B alone or with one or more partners, your role as host will be multifaceted. It begins when you first say hello to a prospective guest who has called to inquire about your B&B. You'll need to keep a reservation calendar, send out written confirmations, and supply good directions. Once guests have checked in, they will rely on you for information about what there is to see and do in the area, restaurant suggestions, directions, and a myriad of other details. You will be responsible—directly, or indirectly if you have hired help—for making sure that the guest rooms and bathrooms are clean and welcoming; that the food served is delicious and well prepared; that the dining room is attractive and inviting; that the common rooms are well appointed, well lit, and comfortable; that fresh flower arrangements are *fresh;* that the outside of the B&B is as appealing as the inside; that your bookkeeping is accurate and up-to-date; that permits and licenses are in order—and on and on.

As you can see, the owner of a B&B is a busy person, acting as reservation agent, receptionist, bookkeeper, chambermaid, host, interior decorator, cook, waitress, and local tourism expert. A larger B&B can justify having hired help, but outside help is usually limited, and even so, the primary responsibility for keeping everything running smoothly rests with the host/owner/operator—you. And most B&Bs are simply not large enough (and thereby profitable enough) to warrant hiring a cook, for instance, or sending out the laundry. Therefore, the B&B host must be a jack-of-all-trades—not to mention well organized and energetic.

The Bed-and-Breakfast Itself

As experienced B&B travelers know, houses that are now bed-and-breakfasts represent every architectural style to be found. Even if you haven't yet done much B&B exploring, a glimpse through a good guidebook will quickly introduce you to exquisite mansions of graceful proportions, furnished with stunning period antiques; cozy bungalows furnished with solid pieces from the Arts and Crafts era; a log cabin with hand-hewn beams; an airy Victorian with a wicker-furnished porch; or an elegant brownstone with marble fireplaces. The types of houses, and the furnishings within, are of an almost infinite variety. Indeed, this variety, which sets B&Bs apart from other commercial lodgings, is proving to be an essential part of their appeal to the traveling public. New or old, large or small, there is no single "right" style of house for a bed-and-breakfast; if the house is comfortable, attractive, and in a good location, just about any house will do.

The settings of B&Bs range from small coastal towns to ski resorts, college communities, residential neighborhoods, major cities, and rural farms. Across America, B&Bs can increasingly be found in nearly any locale, as would-be hosts recognize the demand and dedicated B&B travelers fill the rooms.

As you might imagine, the decor of each bed-and-breakfast—along with the food served and the other amenities offered—will be as varied as the architecture and settings of the buildings themselves. But regardless of style, the decor of the rooms will be much prettier than any hotel or motel could be. In the guest rooms, beds may be made with patchwork quilts and elegant comforters, and plump, down-filled pillows in snowy, starched linen shams; the bed itself may be an antique—canopied, four-poster, or old iron. There is *nothing* in the room that is reminiscent of the unmistakable standard hotel-style quilted bedspread and institutional furniture. The dining room and common rooms may be furnished with family heirlooms, furniture, rugs, and objets d'art that, old or new, combine to create the unique ambiance of that particular B&B. Inevitably, there is a homey, cozy feeling in a bed-and-breakfast that simply cannot be found in a hotel or motel. This atmosphere is a large part of what American travelers are falling in love with.

The food served at breakfast is home-cooked, and the aromas of coffee and baked goods drift up to the rooms as guests awaken. Breakfast is offered in settings designed to make the guests feel pampered—in a traditional dining room, on a garden patio, or in front of a crackling fireplace, to name but a few. The china, cutlery, glassware, and linens are all part of a meal designed to be as memorable and special as possible. In today's world of fast-food restaurants, Americans are starved for this kind of service and attention to detail.

I believe it is this emphasis on personal service, delivered directly by the host to each guest, that is making the B&B traveler feel welcomed and pampered in a way that is not matched at other lodging establishments. A gracious host is as much a part of the special memories of a vacation as is the destination itself.

All of these factors—the unique beauty and charm of each house, the settings, the home-cooked food served with pride and care, and the attention of a concerned and gracious host—have contributed to making B&B stays the hottest trend in lodging for traveling Americans.

The Business Side of the "Dream Job"

Probably the most important point I can make for those considering starting a bed-and-breakfast is that a B&B is a relatively small, home-based *business.* You must remember that. It can be a fun, interesting, and pleasant way to make money, but there is work involved. In order to make a profit, you must do much of the work of running the B&B yourself; otherwise the income (gross receipts) will be used up paying others to do the day-to-day chores.

Many hosts make a conscious choice to leave an outside job and work at home running a B&B. If you will be doing that, it's important to realize that you are still *working.* When I first started my B&B, friends and acquaintances would say things to me like, "Since you're not working, I was hoping you could help us with this project by volunteering to lobby at the state house"; "Now that you're not working, we thought you'd want to have the reunion dinner at your house"; "Since you're home now, I was hoping to leave the kids with you while I go shopping," and so on. At first I was so caught off guard that I would agree to commitments I really didn't have the time or desire to keep. Gradually I learned politely but firmly to remind such callers that I was still employed—self-employed! You will have to make it clear to family and friends that even though you are working at home, you are working! Just as no one would drop in on you unexpectedly at your office, whether to visit, ask a favor, or drop off a child to be watched, so too your home must now be respected as your place of work.

Common Misconceptions

To bring running a B&B into focus as a job, let's look at some common misconceptions:

Running a B&B is like being on vacation, sitting around conversing with your guests.

First of all, most guests don't expect or want to sit around and chat with the host for any substantial amount of time. In any case, you will be too busy to sit for hours on end socializing: you will have beds to make, rooms to clean, laundry to wash and fold and put away, ironing, grocery shopping, banking, and bookkeeping, to name just a few regular chores, not to mention finding time for your own life! Although what most hosts put high on the list of what they like best about running a B&B is getting to meet so many interesting people from around the world, good hosts have learned to balance the socializing with the mundane but necessary chores that keep the B&B going.

Running a B&B is not a real job.

Running a B&B is a real job, but people—including guests—often don't realize it. During my first year of business a couple came to stay with me without a reservation; they had seen my sign and stopped. I showed them the room, described the full breakfast, and quoted them the rate. At the time, my rate for double occupancy was forty dollars per night. (The local motels were charging sixty dollars, and the local hotel started at one hundred dollars without breakfast.) The wife was thrilled and wanted to stay; the husband wanted a discount, but I explained that if they were only staying for one night, I could not lower the rate. To make a long story short, they ended up staying, but as they left the following morning, I heard the husband say to his wife as they walked down the steps of our front porch, "Forty dollars! And all she has to do is change the sheets!" I thought to myself, "Boy, oh boy, mister, are you wrong!"

Running a B&B is all profit.

The expenses of running a B&B include the obvious—the food served at breakfast, the cost of laundering bed linens and bath towels, and the cost of hired help, if you have any. The not-so-obvious costs are the hot water used by guests, the cost of heating or cooling guest rooms, added insurance, the sheets and towels themselves (they don't last forever!), the mattresses and box springs (ditto!), bath soaps, tissue, toilet paper, cleaning supplies, brochures, business cards, advertising, stamps, envelopes, stationery, long-distance phone calls, flowers, and so on. All of this overhead cuts into the gross amount you make every season.

A young couple from Utah who stayed at my B&B years ago (at a rate of sixty dollars for the night) made me laugh in the morning when they confided that they had calculated how much money I was making and were considering getting into the business. According to them, since I had "spent only about two hours" taking care of them, I must be making about thirty dollars an hour! They hadn't even considered the cost of the breakfast and the loaf of homemade bread they were taking with them, not to mention the planning and advertising I had done to reach them in Utah! But the intangible that guests are really paying for is your time. As you will quickly learn, that is the most valuable commodity of your business.

All the guests are marvelous people.

In general, travelers who frequent B&Bs are a very nice bunch. Often well traveled and well read, they are of all ages and from a variety of interesting professions. They are a bit adventuresome, they like interaction with other travelers, and they don't care about a TV in their room. That said, it is inevitable that you will get an unpleasant guest sleeping under your roof at some point. You must be prepared to accept that and still be gracious and hospitable. You cannot let a sour guest rankle you and affect your treatment of other guests. Most commonly, the worst complaint B&B hosts have about undesirable guests is rudeness. From my own experience, I'd have to say that rude, thoughtless behavior is the worst problem.

Here is an example: Although I have two seatings, or times, when breakfast is served (it's a full breakfast), I try to be flexible and accommodate guests who need an earlier breakfast in order to make an early ferry, plane, or what have you. If guests want to eat as early as, say, 7:00 A.M., I generally offer them a continental-plus breakfast—fresh fruit, a baked item, juice, coffee or tea, and cereal. It's not the full breakfast I serve later, but it's fine for *nearly* everyone. One summer, however, I had a gentleman I just couldn't please. He had asked for a discount, since he was reserving two rooms and staying for three nights while he, his wife, and daughter were coming to town to enroll the daughter at the local university. Although it was peak season and I could have easily filled the rooms at my highest rate, I gave them the discount thinking, "If they like it here, this family will be coming back at least twice a year for the next four years." Once they arrived, I soon discovered that the discounted rate had just been the beginning. These people continually asked me to change my way of doing things to suit them. After forty-eight hours of constant demands without ever so much as a thank-you, I couldn't wait for them to leave. On their last day, the father informed me that they would have to eat breakfast the next day at 7:30 A.M. in order to leave in time for their flight home. When I described the breakfast I would have for them, he became quite nasty, insisting on the full breakfast that he had "paid for" and that had been part of the reason they chose my B&B.

Nowadays I would calmly stand my ground, but then I was still a bit green and foolishly thought I wanted repeat business from this ogre! I caved in and agreed to the full breakfast, and to make things easier on myself prepared a breakfast casserole soufflé that is assembled the day before and baked in the morning. I planned for the casserole to be ready exactly at 7:30, but of course my guests were in the dining room a little after 7:00, rudely informing me that they were ready for breakfast "now." I explained that breakfast would be ready at 7:30, as we had agreed, and that was the best I could do for them. At this point, I was seething with anger and starting to have second thoughts about running a B&B at all. Another couple was due down for breakfast shortly, so I had to force myself to stay calm. I breathed a huge sigh of relief when the family left that morning, but my real satisfaction came a couple of months later, when that same gentleman called to make another reservation and I was able to tell him, pleasantly of course, that I did not have any rooms available, even though I did.

When you have guests who are trying the limits of your patience, tell yourself that they will soon be gone and that you don't need ever to have them stay at your B&B again. You *will* remember their name, and when they call for a reservation you can take pleasure in finding that your calendar is full.

***Because you're working at home,
you have lots of time for your own interests.***

If you've fantasized about running your own B&B and finally devoting yourself to writing that novel, making those dried wreaths (patchwork quilts, rag dolls, boat models—insert your hobby here) on a full-time basis, think again! Once your B&B becomes established, you'll find yourself extremely busy running it and will have to schedule specific times for other activities. For instance, during the peak season of each year I have full occupancy at my B&B for about three months straight. Ninety consecutive days without a day off can be hard to take at any job, even running a B&B! And with that level of business activity it's easy to let your own personal activities get squeezed out. What to do? Make a realistic schedule for yourself and follow it, as much as possible. If getting up an hour earlier each morning will do the trick, then see to it that you take that hour. The rewards will be worth the effort. If you are more productive in the afternoon, consider hiring a teenager a few days a week to answer the phone, the door, etc., while you have two uninterrupted hours to yourself. You get the picture. Although you will need to be very flexible if you are going to succeed in this business, you must carve out a niche of time that's yours and yours alone—every day or on a set number of days each week—or you will quickly tire of the constant demands made of you in this seven-day-a-week profession.

With those misconceptions cleared up, you should now have a better idea of the reality of running a B&B. If you're the right person for the job, it's a wonderful way to work at home and to meet some fascinating people in the process.

Pluses and Minuses

At this point it's a good idea to make a list of the pluses and minuses. Here's my list, but you may want to rearrange some of the items, moving them from one column to the other. You may also want to add a few of your own. And only you can decide how much weight to give to any plus or minus on the list. What's barely significant to me may be of great importance to you.

Pluses

work at home
gain income and tax advantages while restoring an old house
meet interesting people
no commuting required
no suits required
no panty hose or high heels required
no sitting at a desk or phone all day
be your own boss
start or increase a complementary or spin-off business
make your own schedule
get away from unpleasant coworkers/supervisors/bosses

Minuses

loss of privacy
many seven-day work weeks
sharing house with strangers
loss of paid benefits
self-employment taxes
less structured schedule
cabin fever
loss of camaraderie of coworkers
frequent interruptions
rude guests

Let's look at some of these in more detail. I find working at home a delightful choice, especially after years of working a forty-hour week in an office. But many of my friends say they wouldn't want to work at home because they would be tempted to visit the fridge all day and snack, they like having someone else make their schedule, and they like their paid vacations. Working at home is not a plus for everyone. Even if it is a plus for you, sooner or later cabin fever sets in (see the minus list) and you will be desperate to get away from home!

I was very glad to give up commuting and my office wardrobe, but for some the trade-off of buying their own health insurance, paying self-employment taxes, and making their own retirement plan is not worth it. The loss of privacy is a real issue, but how much weight you give it is a very individual matter. I've found ways to lessen the loss of privacy, but I'm not a person who minds terribly finding near-strangers sitting in my living room. For some people, however, the need for privacy makes running a B&B the wrong choice.

Go through the exercise of making your own list, and talk with your spouse or partner about his or her ideas of the pluses and minuses. This is the first step in deciding if running a B&B is the right choice for you. I once met a host who found she loved running a B&B, but her husband, who continued to work outside the home, was so disturbed by the loss of privacy that she was finally forced to close the business. It's important that all concerned parties take a long, hard look at what they'll be getting into.

What's in It for Me?

Why does anyone decide to run a bed-and-breakfast? The reasons are as varied as each B&B. Perhaps it's an enterprise you've dreamed of trying after retirement. If you have a comfortable retirement income and no longer have a mortgage on your house, and have enjoyed B&B stays as travelers yourselves, opening a B&B offers an interesting way to meet other travelers, stay active, and earn a little extra money in the process.

Or perhaps you're a young couple who long to get away from the rat race of your present jobs. You enjoy B&B lodging when you travel and want to try running a B&B because it appears to be so much fun. You may also see it as a way to justify purchasing a beautiful big old house—larger than you would ever need if you did not operate a B&B.

For some hosts, opening a B&B seems like the best tie-in with the work they are already doing at home. If you are already self-employed in the field of catering, restoring and selling antiques, handcrafts, computer consulting, free-lance writing, landscape design, or farming, to name just a few, running a B&B can be a fulfilling complementary profession.

If you live in a seasonal resort area, running a B&B complements certain occupations, such as teaching, very well indeed. With school vacations and free time in the summer, you may find that opening your home to B&B travelers fits into your schedule now on a part-time basis and is something to look forward to as a full-time occupation after retirement, with a clientele already established.

Perhaps you see running a B&B as an opportunity to earn money while still being home with your young children. This is certainly working well for a number of hosts I've met, though quite often the husband continues to work outside the home.

For the parent who has decided to stay at home while the children are young, running a B&B (with hired help, of course) allows her to be there to send her kids off to school in the morning, greet them when they come home from school, nurse them when they are home from school with an illness, attend school functions, etc., and still earn a little money—all the while building a business that she can expand when her children are older, if she so desires. For the parent of preschool children, running a B&B is a bit more tricky because these kids are home all day and require more attention. But it is possible, as hosts I know personally will attest. While it's true that children can be noisy and demanding at inconvenient times—and this could be a liability for a B&B host—the parent who wants to make this work, can. The house must be sufficiently large and she must have reliable hired help. And she must be sharp enough to know that travelers are not coming to her B&B to get to know her child.

If you have sufficient income from other investments (rental properties, for example), and have found a sizable house (at *least* six guest rooms) in an area with potential year-round B&B business, then perhaps both you and your partner plan on running the B&B full-time. These circumstances can be very satisfactory financially and still allow time for one or both of you to pursue another home-based business.

In addition to the income you will earn from running a bed-and-breakfast, there are numerous tax advantages, which may be as or more important to you than the income itself. You will be able to deduct certain expenses on your tax return that you would be incurring whether you had the B&B or not but that now are deductible because of your business—which is also producing income! If you don't already, you should have an accountant help you with your tax return once you start a B&B, and he or she should be well versed in all the applicable deductions. Even so, attend one of the many B&B tax advantage seminars given by accountants specializing in this field. You'll probably pick up some good information to share with your accountant. (Chapter 10 contains more specifics about some of the most common deductions available.)

As you can see, the reasons for starting a bed-and-breakfast, and the possibilities of combining other occupations with B&B hosting, are many and varied. My advice is to keep your options as wide as possible.

The Bottom Line

The amount of money you can make running a B&B varies widely as well, depending on the number of guest rooms, the level of business in the area, whether or not the business is seasonal, and what you can reasonably charge for your rooms. Chapter 8 will help you decide how to set your room rates, but for the purpose of an example, let's say that you have a B&B with four guest rooms and you are charging $80 per night per room. A fairly accurate way to calculate an average season's (or year's) gross income for your B&B, once it is established, is to multiply your per-night full-occupancy gross by one hundred nights. For an example, four rooms at $80 each per night is $320 per night at full occupancy. Multiplying by a hundred nights gives you a gross of $32,000. Remember, this figure is a gross, and we have not deducted operating (or start-up) expenses. With the mortgage you currently have, and other living expenses, could you live on this amount (or whatever amount your calculation yields)? If your employer is paying your health insurance, you need to add that expense— and it's sizable—into your cost-of-living budget. (Although the future of health insurance is uncertain at the moment, most individuals leaving the employ of a company to start their own B&B will face the sizable expense of procuring their own health insurance. Under the latest proposals for reform, the best prospects for the self-employed are slightly lower rates because the pool of insured would be larger, and more importantly, the ability to deduct 100 percent of the expense at tax time.) And remember that when you're working for yourself, there's no guaranteed, regular paycheck; business can be boom or bust.

For these reasons I encourage couples considering quitting their jobs to run a B&B to go about it slowly and cautiously. It's really best if one of the two continues to work outside the home, for the financial security an outside job offers. Also, the first year in business will probably be a slim one: you'll be spending money on necessary start-up expenses but not yet getting much business, because the traveling public doesn't know you're there.

Start-up Costs

Most B&B hosts, unless they have purchased an existing, successful B&B, will not be making much profit for the first year or even two years, depending on the amount of money needed to ready the house for business. These start-up costs are an important reason for would-be hosts to consider how they could make money from another source while running their B&B, for the first year or two especially. Perhaps you can continue to work at your present job, but on a part-time basis, while you establish your B&B and see firsthand if it's really a business you want to be in for the long haul.

There are exceptions to every rule, and the exceptions here are couples who are purchasing an existing bed-and-breakfast, and couples with sufficient income from other sources not to rely on the B&B income to support themselves.

If you are considering buying an existing bed-and-breakfast (and there are some very tempting listings every month in the trade publications; see the appendix, page 181, for resources), you may be virtually guaranteed a good income right from the start. This income will be reduced by your mortgage and other regular operating expenses, but you will not have the initial start-up expenses that someone starting a B&B from scratch will have.

It is impossible to come up with an exact figure for start-up costs because each house will have different requirements. The costs of renovations will vary in different parts of the country, and the kind of materials you want used will affect the price as well. Redoing an existing bathroom, for instance, can cost hundreds of dollars or thousands, depending on whether you install a vinyl or ceramic tile floor, a fiberglass or custom-tiled shower stall, a vanity topped with Formica or marble, and so on. If you are able to do some of the work yourself—painting, wallpapering, plumbing, or wiring—your start-up costs will be less than if you contract out all the work. But whether you plan on doing much of the work yourself or not, knowing which items are musts for this business should help you determine what *your* start-up expenses will be at the very least. Assuming that your house and guest rooms are in good condition, you will need

- beds in top condition
- adequate bedding in top condition
- new bath towels
- blinds or shades for the windows
- smoke detectors in each room
- attractive china, glassware, and cutlery for breakfast
- business cards and brochures
- advertising

These are the bare-bones basics; there is much more that you can and should add later. But you may be better off starting with just these if that's all that's within your budget. It is a mistake to spend too much before you find out if this business is right for you and before you find out if the business will repay you for these expenses. Chapter 10 gives specific tips on figuring how much to spend when you first open your B&B.

Making the Leap

I hope it is becoming clear that this *can* be a flexible occupation, either allowing you to make a little extra money or becoming your primary source of income. You can tailor this occupation to work for you.

If after weighing the pros and cons you decide that running a B&B is something you'd like to try, you will find specific tips in the chapters that follow to lessen the minuses and strengthen the pluses and to help you eventually become the successful, happy bed-and-breakfast owner you dream of being.

2

The Bed-and-Breakfast House

> *L*et me live in my house by
> the side of the road and be a
> friend to man.
> —SAM WALTER FOSS

Location, Location, Location

*I*f you're going to be buying a house for your bed-and-breakfast enterprise rather than using your current home, your first consideration will be location. Once you've decided on the area of the country you'd like to live in, you need to assess whether the business the area offers is potentially year-round or seasonal. For instance, if you currently live in Los Angeles and dream of moving to ski country in Colorado, you must ask yourself if there are reasons that travelers would come to the area other than to ski. The proximity of a college or university is a plus, since there will be parents, prospective students and professors, lecturers, and the like coming to the area to visit the school during most of the year—thereby stretching your season beyond the ski months. Hosts of a B&B I know of in the Hanover, New Hampshire, area have found business there to be much more year-round than they originally anticipated. They are, of course, very busy during the winter months because of their proximity to good ski areas, but the fall foliage brings just as much business their way, and their closeness to Dartmouth College has provided them with steady business bookings during what they thought might be slow months.

Ask yourself if the area attracts primarily pleasure or business travelers or some combination of both. As the Hanover, New Hampshire, example illustrates, a combination of both is ideal, since it gives you the potential for more clientele. There may be ups and downs in vacation travel, but business travel tends to remain steady. It may not be a university that brings in your business travelers; perhaps your B&B will be near an important hospital or clinic, or the headquarters of a major corporation, or a small but thriving business that has dealings nationwide. If you don't already know what potential business your area offers, contact the chamber of commerce.

You may know what you like about the area you've selected, but does the traveling public have a reason to like it too? Your business cannot succeed if travelers are not going to be attracted to the region, and in fairly good numbers, or if the area is too difficult to reach.

That said, don't underestimate the market for unusual, specialty locations. A couple I met at one of my seminars showed me the plans for their dream B&B, which they were having built in Arizona. He was retiring from a university career, and both were avid bird-watchers, or birders. They had spent many vacations visiting places where birding was the main attraction, and their favorite had been in a fairly remote section of Arizona. They had done their homework and had impressive figures on and mailing lists of fellow bird and nature enthusiasts. Although their location was one that would be unfamiliar to many, I'm certain their B&B is a success.

Another one of my favorite B&Bs is set in a wonderfully remote part of Wyoming. This B&B is also a ranch, and in addition to providing a setting of hundreds of acres of incredible natural beauty, there is horseback riding, skiing in winter, and real western rodeos to attend. With the proper advertising, this B&B has made a niche for itself. Whatever area you choose, chances are there are reasons travelers will be coming through.

Or perhaps you're going to stay in the town you've lived in for the last twenty years. It isn't famous for anything in particular, but you think it has lots of charm. If it's a location you love, and one that makes you happy, you can probably find a way to get others to discover it too.

Last but not least, whatever you decide to promote as special about your location—in your brochures, advertising, etcetera—be accurate. It is far better for your guests to be pleasantly surprised by how marvelous your setting truly is than for you to raise their expectations unrealistically high and then disappoint them. I've heard this complaint from other travelers, and it has happened to me too. I once made a reservation at a B&B that advertised an "on the lake" location. In reality, they were separated from the lake by a busy street, and the jogging path they told me about was a dangerously narrow shoulder. Because they had not been honest, I was let down before I even saw my room—not a good way to start off a B&B stay.

Curb Appeal

After location, the house itself is the single most important factor in the business and your largest investment. Assuming that your location is one that draws visitors—whether for business or pleasure—the house must be appealing and comfortable, or your business won't fly. This aesthetic aspect is referred to by real estate agents as "curb appeal." You know, the kind of house that makes you slow down and stare as you drive by it. The kind of house that you want to move into, or at least be allowed to stay at for a brief visit.

If you have any experience with restoration, you can probably look at a house in disrepair and see the potential for it to be a gem. Many folks who have beautiful B&Bs today started with houses in terrible shape. Along the way, they recorded the restoration in a photo album—a fun item to share with interested guests—and the tax advantages and B&B income helped pay for the transformation.

Sometimes all a house needs is a new coat of paint and a little yard work. A well-tended flower bed at the front of the house can add tremendous visual appeal. Even a modest bungalow becomes an inviting retreat when surrounded by a well-tended lawn nicely planted with trees, shrubs, and perennial borders.

Or add a special punch with a lively shade of paint on your front door. That detail, along with changing, seasonal wreaths and an artistic B&B sign, may just make your B&B a local landmark.

Whatever the size and style of the house and yard, they should be immediately inviting. All you have to do is imagine what your guests will first see as they approach your B&B; then you will know what needs to be spruced up, redone, or emphasized.

I've heard too many horror stories from fellow travelers about B&Bs that accurately advertised locations where guests would "wake up to the sounds of the surf" or "ski from the front door" but offered houses that were cramped, run-down, and just plain unattractive. Regardless of the superior location, these travelers will never return to those B&Bs and will not be spreading the good reviews that are vital to the success of a bed-and-breakfast. If you open your B&B for business while the restoration is still in progress, as some hosts do, make sure the house is clean and that at least some portion of it is completely ready to show off to your guests. And of course, provide this information to prospective guests when they call.

Zoning: Playing by the Rules

Once you've decided on the general location you want—for instance, a medium-sized town in southern coastal Maine—and narrowed the search

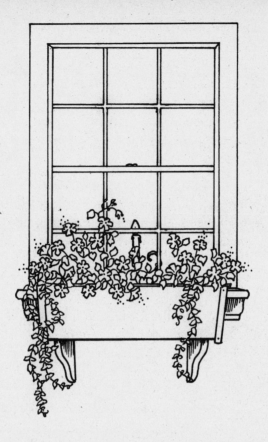

to a few towns, check into the zoning. What each town and state will allow regarding B&B operations varies greatly. Make sure the towns you're interested in will allow you to operate the kind of B&B business you plan on before wasting your time looking at real estate. Contact the town hall *and* the chamber of commerce for information of this sort. This is an important step that you may be tempted to avoid, especially if you've found the "perfect" house in a town whose zoning won't allow a B&B in that particular neighborhood. Don't make the mistake of thinking that you can operate your business discreetly and thereby get around the rules. Sooner or later you could be asked to shut down and even fined.

If the town does allow B&Bs in the neighborhood you've selected, be sure to check out all the nitty-gritty details. For instance, some towns allow bed-and-breakfasts but put a "two double-occupancy rooms only" limit on them. I've met enough hosts from around the country to learn that these limits are very arbitrary. If you're going to start your B&B in the house that you currently live in and you find the zoning too restrictive, you may be able to form a B&B association with other hosts and work to change the zoning. Quite often the persons at the town hall in charge of these matters don't really know what a B&B is.

The Perfect House: Layout and Design

Again, there is no one single right style of house for a bed-and-breakfast. There are, however, certain factors that make some houses better suited than others for this business. Here are some things to consider if you are in the market for a house that will also serve as a B&B:

Guest Rooms

The more guest rooms you have, the more money you can make running your B&B. Depending on what the zoning allows, generally speaking, the more rooms you have, the better. There are reasons to limit yourself, though, other than zoning. Most hosts can operate a two- or three-bedroom B&B by themselves. Once you get to four rooms, with four private baths, you start to need some kind of part-time hired help. A B&B with six, eight, or ten rooms requires, as you can imagine, more than just

part-time help. Although a B&B this size is obviously a much more lucrative enterprise, it is also much more demanding than a small operation. Training and managing a staff is not an easy job. And of course, certain operating expenses, such as insurance, will be higher for a large-capacity B&B. One important advantage of owning a large bed-and-breakfast, however, is that you *will* have full-time help, which makes it easier for you to get away from the business—for an hour or two, or a day, or a weekend. And since you will be able to justify offering your help substantial hours, and therefore a substantial wage each week, it may be easier to find and keep good help. Weigh all these considerations carefully when shopping for the ideal house. You are the only one who can decide just how large a B&B you want to run.

It is ideal to have guest rooms that do not share walls with other guest rooms. Sound impossible? It isn't; hallways, bathrooms, and closets can allow for this arrangement. If the bedrooms do share common walls, plan on installing sound insulation when you renovate. If the house is quite old, the bedrooms may not have closets. In this case you will need armoires. And the size of some bedrooms in older houses can be a problem; you'll want even the smallest room to comfortably hold a double or queen-sized bed. The guest rooms needn't be spacious—although if they are, so much the better—but they will need to hold all the necessary furniture and still allow your guests to move about the room with ease. Very small rooms, however, can sometimes be connected to larger ones, allowing you to offer suites. A suite should provide a bedroom, sitting room, and bathroom. If you are able to make one or more of your guest rooms into suites, you will be at an advantage: travelers will pay more for suites, and the couch in the sitting room can convert to a bed, making this a room for children to use as a bedroom at night. If you are going to accommodate families with children, suites can be ideal, especially if the sitting room has a TV. That way, kids who might be disruptive in a common room—where other guests are trying to read or write postcards or what have you—can have fun without disturbing anyone.

Bathrooms

Nowadays B&B travelers want private baths. If the house you've fallen in love with doesn't have separate baths for all the bedrooms, could they be added? In some older houses large linen closets, dressing rooms, or tiny bedrooms can be converted into full baths (more about this in chapter 4). It may be more realistic to supply only some rooms with private full baths while others have a private half bath (sink and toilet) with a shared full bath down the hall. Baths that *are* shared should not be shared by more than two rooms.

Common Rooms

You'll need to provide your guests with more than just a bedroom and bathroom. B&B travelers expect to have access to a living room. Ideally, it should not be the only living room in the house, as you and your family will want to be able to relax without being with guests. Look for a house with a family room, or the potential for one to be added; off the kitchen is a good location.

Master Bedroom Location

Your bedroom should not abut any guest rooms, if possible. You need some distance for your privacy as well as theirs. The ideal house would have a separate wing for the host's quarters—bedroom, bath, and living room. And if the house has two stairways, the hallway leading to the back stairs should be adjacent to your private part of the house.

General Layout

Whether the house is grand or modest, there should be some sense of space and privacy, for you and your guests. A house that feels cramped to you will be unsuitable for paying guests. If you're in the market for a fairly sizable house, look for one with a main staircase and a back stairway. Usually virtually hidden to guests, back stairs become a convenient way for you and your helpers to dash through the house unnoticed. A house with two living rooms is ideal for a B&B; one could be for you and your family and the other for guests. Or both could be for guests, one being home to a TV, the other more suitable for quiet relaxation. In this case you would have your own sitting room tucked away and hidden from guests, perhaps part of a master bedroom suite. If you are going to run your B&B while your

children still live at home, you *must* have a separate family room. If the house doesn't have one, plan on an addition. After all, your children still need to be able to have friends over without disrupting your business. You'll want a good-sized dining room, separated from the kitchen by a door that you can close. And the kitchen should be large enough for some serious cooking if you plan to offer a full breakfast and a full house is twelve guests. Old houses usually have pantries, wonderful for storage. Porches, sun rooms, patios, and decks are all wonderful assets to the B&B home; these become special areas for guests or private places for just you. If you find a property that includes a carriage house or barn, you may decide to turn that into your living quarters, making the house entirely a B&B. Or you may decide to set up the barn to accommodate families with children, or large groups, to provide them with some privacy. An outbuilding can serve as a home to your other business—antiques, say—or as living quarters for your hired help during peak season. A host I know with a B&B near a large university uses her barn apartment as a student rental from September to June and then uses the rooms as extra B&B rooms during her busy summer season. Or you and your family may camp out in the barn while the main house undergoes restoration and remodeling before opening for business.

Cosmetics

Unless you're buying an existing B&B, you'll probably want to do some painting and wallpapering. If you can do any of that work yourself, so much the better. You'll save money and enjoy talking with guests later about how you did it. But whether you do the work yourself or not, the expense of extensive cosmetic work is an important consideration in calculating start-up costs. Be realistic about how much of this you can afford to do before opening for business.

General Condition

If you're buying an old house, you'll want to make sure the electrical, septic, and heating systems are all capable of handling the operation you plan on, and if they are not, you'll want to be certain they can be properly modified. The typical eighty-gallon hot water heater is *not* going to be sufficient. And if you were to add three more bathrooms, what would happen to the water pressure? Does the house have different heating zones or just one? If you're going to be open during the winter months, you'll want as many separate heating zones as possible. What's the sound insulation like: can you hear every word your husband says to you from the next room? Does the roof leak? And what condition are the windows in; will they need to be replaced? Are there storm windows? You'll need to get together with a reliable contractor to discuss these issues.

Parking

Unless you are going to open a B&B in a large city, you will need to provide off-street parking for your guests. If the house does not currently have a parking area, could one be tastefully added? Off-street parking is important for two reasons: First of all, your guests will feel their cars are safer when they are parked off the street. Secondly, numerous cars clogging a residential street and blocking neighbors' driveways are a sure way to get your neighbors upset about your B&B. I know of a bed-and-breakfast that was shut down over this very issue by a well-documented complaint brought by a group of disgruntled neighbors. Your parking area should have enough room for one car for each guest room, plus your cars, unless they will be parked in a garage.

The Yard

A yard for guests' use is not a necessity, but it is a big plus. Look for a house with a lot providing a private yard for you and your family and

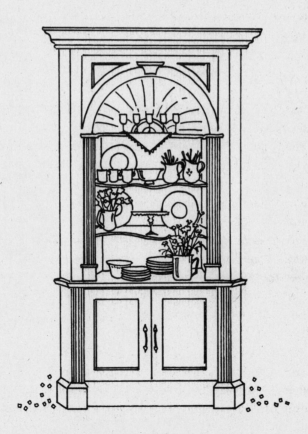

another area that would be appealing to guests. You may not think that you need a separate yard for your use, but you will once you've been in business awhile! If you have found the perfect house and it has only a small back yard, which will be just for you, perhaps a front porch could be added for guests. Our house has a front porch that stretches the width of the house. During the warm weather it's furnished with French café furniture and bedecked with large hanging baskets of fuchsia. It's pretty but nothing terribly special. Still, to my guests from big cities—New York, Boston, Philadelphia—it is a cool, green haven. They are thrilled to be able to sit out there in the morning with their first cup of coffee (or later in the day with a tall glass of iced tea) and enjoy the air and the greenery. Little things like a nice porch go a long way in providing special memories of a place.

This list is meant to serve as a guide to help you in your search for your bed-and-breakfast house. The perfect house probably doesn't exist, but all of these are important considerations to keep in mind.

We did not buy our house with a bed-and-breakfast operation in mind. Nevertheless, it is a graceful old house and we have made it work well for my small business. If we were to buy a house specifically for a B&B, I would hold out for a house that had all (or nearly all) the features mentioned so far: a separate wing with a master bedroom suite; two stairways; two living rooms for guests; and two porches—one for guests, one for us.

In any case, choose a house that *you* will enjoy living in. You may have to sacrifice some of the items on your wish list in order to afford the house with the three-acre yard. But if the yard means more to you than having a master bedroom suite, you'll probably be happy with the trade-off. If you love the house, your guests will know it, and they will be more likely to find it special too.

Buyer Beware: What to Look For If You Buy an Existing B&B

There are many thriving B&Bs offered for sale each year, and the real estate listings in the trade publications provide information on businesses large and small in every region of the country. One of the obvious advantages of buying an existing B&B is that you should be able to make a profit from it right away. The house will already be set up as a bed-and-breakfast, and there should be an established clientele. Although you may want to make some changes to the house itself, an existing B&B is what is called a "turn-key" operation by real estate agents: you simply turn the key, walk in, and you're in business. This means, of course, that the house will cost more than if it were simply a private home. But that extra expense may be worth it to you if it's the ideal house in the town of your dreams. Before you buy, however, you (or your representative) must ask some hard questions of the prospective sellers—no matter how good it all looks at first glance.

Your first question should be, "Why are you selling?" The answer may simply be that the business has become too much for a couple past retirement age. Then again, it may be that the business has never really afforded the couple the living they thought it would and they're having trouble meeting the mortgage. If this is the case (and you'll have to do some sleuthing to find out), ask yourself why things would be any different for you. Perhaps the house *would* work for you because you'd have a smaller mortgage or you have other investments and sources of income.

You will need to ask if there is a lawsuit pending. If there is, get your lawyer to advise you on your liability if you were to buy the B&B before the suit was resolved.

You and your accountant must make a thorough examination of the establishment's books, going back at least three years or as long as the sellers have owned the B&B. If there has been a decline in business, ask why. Perhaps something as uncontrollable as bad weather has been responsible for the slip in bookings, but if business has dropped off due to shoddy standards, you'll have some work to do to restore the B&B's reputation: you will practically be starting from scratch in building a new clientele. One good way to determine guest satisfaction with an existing B&B is to send a simple questionnaire to a random sampling from the mailing list. This will take some time, but the effort will pay off both in your decision whether to buy the B&B and in your assessment of what improvements to make if you do.

Is the success of the business based on something like a good snowfall? If it is, be prepared for the occasional off winter, when Mother Nature doesn't provide good snow conditions, and ask yourself how you would

survive that kind of loss of income. It's always safer (but obviously not a necessity) to find an area of the country that offers year-round attractions.

Find out the status of future bookings and deposits. Those monies should be transferred to you if you do buy the business, or negotiated in the selling price.

With these questions, and the help of your lawyer and accountant, you should be able to choose an existing B&B whose business will soar under your ownership.

Turning Your Current House into a B&B

You may decide, now that your children have grown, that your house would make a great bed-and-breakfast. That may be true, but you still need to ask yourself the same questions as someone shopping for a house:

- What's special about your location?
- Does the house have curb appeal?
- What does the local zoning allow?
- Is the layout and design of your house well suited for paying guests? Will you and your guests have privacy from one another?
- Will you need to add bathrooms?
- What is the general condition of your house? Take a close look; it probably needs cosmetic work at the least.
- Will you need to add a second hot water tank? Will your septic system stand the extra use? How many heat zones does the house have?

In other words, whether you are considering converting your house or shopping for a new house or an existing B&B, the considerations are virtually the same.

3
The Bed-and-Breakfast Bedroom

The Well-Appointed Guest Room

*T*he phrase "bed and breakfast" subtly implies that there is something special about the guest quarters and brings to mind a bedroom that is cozy, intimate, and inviting. This is exactly what your guest rooms should be—restful havens for the weary traveler. They may even go so far as being elegant, as they do in many B&Bs, but they certainly will be a world apart from the standard motel or hotel room. While the rooms in motels and hotels all have a certain sameness—a homogenized, anonymous look—the guest rooms at bed-and-breakfasts are unique, appealing, and stamped with a definitive character, as individual as each host. As you know from staying at B&Bs yourself, this charm is certainly part of what you look forward to when making your reservation and part of what would cause you to recommend a particular B&B to friends.

The Necessities

Before your rooms can be charming, they must contain the basics for B&B success. Although you may someday want to wallpaper your guest bedrooms, install custom drapes, and add canopy beds, you don't need all that to start. What you *do* need for each guest room, whether you are converting your children's rooms or purchasing a house for the purpose of starting a B&B, are:

A Top-quality Bed

Don't assume that the twenty-year old mattress that your child never complained about is fine for your B&B. A good night's sleep is extremely important to the traveler, and the quality of your beds will affect your business. Be sure the beds are of superior quality, and with equally good mattresses, box springs, and frames. Guests will not want to return to a bed-and-breakfast where the beds were soft, lumpy, and sagging. Nor will they recommend your B&B to friends. Also, knowing that your beds are top quality, you can be comfortable charging higher rates.

The beds in your double-occupancy rooms should be either queen-sized, king-sized, or two of twin size. I recommend that you have at least one room furnished with two twin-sized beds for those travelers who want to share a room but not a bed—for instance, a mother and daughter, two women friends, siblings, or couples who use twin beds at home. The twin beds should be the extra-long size, made for adults. And twin beds can be pushed together and made up as a king-sized bed with the addition of a foam bridge, available in the bedding department of large department stores, making the room with two twin beds even more versatile. Double beds are not considered suitable for double-occupancy rooms today: most couples want at least a queen-sized bed. They *are* handy, though, for small guest rooms which you intend to use only for the single traveler, because they offer an adult more room than a twin-sized bed.

A headboard allows your guests to sit up in bed—to read or watch TV—without pushing themselves away from the wall. Wooden headboards are preferable to upholstered ones because they will clean more easily and last longer. The footboard is optional; tall people often find them restrictive, and they will make it slightly more time-consuming for you to change and make the beds. Canopy beds, sleigh beds, and other antique styles include footboards, but despite the drawbacks mentioned, your guests will be thrilled to find any of these beautiful beds in their rooms.

Attractive, High-quality Bedding

Do not make the guest beds with the old printed sheets of which you have grown tired! The bed should *look* attractive, as well as being truly comfortable. Sheets and pillowcases should be in immaculate condition. White sheets always look fresh and never go out of style as some prints and colors do. Also, if a sheet needs to be replaced due to a stain or tear, you can always match white. And if you use all-cotton, most stains can be bleached out. Cotton sheets are more expensive than polyester or cotton/poly blends, but they will last longer and lend a distinct air of luxury to the bed. If you cannot afford to purchase cotton bed linens when you are just starting in business, gradually add them to your collection as you replace worn-out sheets of cotton-polyester blend. Cotton pillowcases should be ironed. Supply two pillows per person, at the minimum. The pillows themselves may be down, polyester, cotton, or foam-filled, but remember, some people are allergic to down and some to foam. If you love the luxury of a plump, down-filled pillow, then by all means use them in your guest rooms, but keep some cotton batting or polyester-filled pillows in your linen closet to use as substitutes should the need arise.

The beds should be made with the appropriate number of blankets for the climate, with an extra one in the closet or bureau. Dust ruffles and comforters, or bedspreads, should be in good condition, and they and the blankets should be color-coordinated with the room decor. Purchase blankets and bed covers that can be easily laundered at home, if at all possible. It is inevitable that your guests will not all be as careful with the furnishings as you would: they will sit on the beds in their wet bathing suits, sandy and covered with suntan lotion; put their feet on the bed with their shoes on; spill makeup on the bed; have nosebleeds; spill wine; and have every other kind of accident you can imagine. None of this is much of a problem if you can launder the bedding yourself.

Bedside Tables

There should be a bedside table on each side of the bed in the case of a queen- or king-sized; place one between two twin beds or on one side of a double bed to be used in a single-occupancy room. I can't tell you how many places I've stayed where this piece of furniture was missing, and it always surprises me, especially in an otherwise very satisfactory B&B. Guests need bedside tables for reading glasses, books, clocks, a box of tissues, and so on. Supply a flashlight for emergencies in the top drawer of each bedside table, and be sure your guests know it's there. Check the batteries when you do your cleaning.

Good Lights

There should be reading lights at the beds, either mounted strategically on the wall at either side of a queen- or king-sized bed (at one side of a twin) or on the bedside table. Wall-mounted lights are more convenient since they aren't taking up space on the bedside table, can't be knocked over, and are usually at a more suitable height for reading than bedside lamps. The reading lights should have three-way bulbs for best reading illumination. There should also be good overhead lighting in the room.

Dresser, Bureau, or Chest of Drawers

This piece of furniture may not actually get much use, but it should nevertheless be completely empty, and the drawers lined with paper. The drawers should open and close easily and supply enough storage space for guests who stay an entire week.

Bed Linens

This is the minimum you will need for each guest bed. The duplicates allow you to quickly ready the room for new guests even when there has been a disaster in the room.

2 mattress covers

3 sets of sheets, both fitted and flat

2 pillows per person: 2 for a twin bed, 4 for a queen-sized bed, exception: 6 for a king-sized

2 zippered pillow covers per pillow

3 sets of pillow cases per pillow

2 blankets

2 bedspreads, coverlets, or comforters

2 duvet covers if you are using down comforters

1 dust ruffle

2 sets of pillow shams

*1 throw blanket or down comforter
for foot of bed*

Mirror

There should be a large, well-lit mirror somewhere in the room. If not full-length, it should allow guests a three-quarter view of themselves, so they can see how they look before coming down in the morning, going out to dinner, etc. If the mirror is not directly over the bureau, there should be a stand or small table under or next to it so that guests have a convenient place for hairbrushes and other toiletry items. The inside of a closet door is often a good spot for a full-length mirror, even if there is a smaller one in the room.

Closet or Armoire

The closet or armoire should be *empty,* not used as extra storage for family clothing, as I have too frequently found at B&Bs. It should have a couple of wooden hangers for suits and coats, and the rest of the hangers should be plastic and all of the same make and color. Do *not* use wire hangers! If the closet is large, it should have a light.

Luggage Rack

If you don't supply your guests with luggage racks, they will put their suitcases on the bed. Luggage will soil and tear bed covers, and without a luggage rack, guests are forced to find a spot on the floor for their suitcases when they go to bed. If you have large, walk-in closets, keep the luggage racks in there; this arrangement provides more walking space in the room and keeps the luggage out of sight, so the room looks tidier. Otherwise, place them next to the bureau or at the foot of the bed. Or place a wooden trunk at the foot of the bed: a trunk is very effective as a luggage rack and makes an extra place to sit.

Window Treatments

Windows should have some kind of attractive drapery or curtain, in keeping with the decor of the room, and some kind of shade or blind that allows complete privacy when closed. The windows should open and close easily and have screens.

Smoke Detectors

All guest rooms should have working smoke detectors. Remember to test them on a regular basis to see if the battery needs changing. If the smoke detectors are wired to your electrical system, be sure they are kept clean with a regular vacuuming.

Rugs

I advise against wall-to-wall carpeting since it can so easily become stained and smelly, colors fade and go out of style, and the traffic areas may show wear before you're ready to replace the entire carpet. A wooden floor is always in style, lasts forever (with infrequent refinishing), and is easy to keep clean. With a wooden floor, if you decide to change the color scheme of the room, you don't need to recarpet. Area rugs add a cozy warmth to the room, are easily cleaned, and can greatly enhance the decor. These should always be on nonslip rug pads for your guests' safety.

Clocks

An electric or quartz battery clock should be on the bedside table, so that guests can set an alarm for themselves or at least know what time it is.

House Rules

Establish what your house rules are before you open for business and post them attractively somewhere in the room. Rules include such things as, "Smoking is not allowed in the bedrooms." (More about what your rules should be in chapter 7.) You should be able to limit your house rules to one page. Place the page in some sort of frame to keep the sheet from becoming dog-eared. Some B&Bs like to post the house rules in a picture frame on the inside of the bedroom door, others in a frame standing on the dresser or bedside table.

Electrical Outlets

Each bedroom should have sufficient and conveniently located electrical outlets for your guests' use. Especially if the bath is shared, guests will want to be able to use their hair dryers and electric curlers, etcetera, in their bedroom to avoid spending too much time in the bathroom. And it's a good idea to let guests know you have an ironing board for their use so they don't use their travel iron on top of your antique bureau!

Tissues

Every guest bedroom should have a box of tissues—white, unscented—on the dresser or bedside table. When you are adding the little finishing touches to your rooms, purchase the decorative boxes that are designed to hold and conceal the cardboard tissue box itself.

Wastebasket

Your guest rooms should each have a wastebasket, and not a flimsy one. Purchase wastebaskets that can be rinsed out so that you don't have to use those unattractive and wasteful plastic liners. It may seem extravagant to spend much on a wastebasket, but a pretty one will add to the room's aesthetic appeal and will last longer than a cheap one.

Locks

The bedroom doors should lock from the inside at the very least; a simple slide bolt works well. A lock provides guests with a sense of security and privacy when they are in the room. If your B&B is going to be sizable, you should also have locks that require keys for each guest room so that guests may lock their rooms when they go out. That way guests know that no one else has access to their room except you or your helper. If you do supply locks and keys for the rooms, be sure to keep extra keys on hand; guests will lose them, and you and your helpers will need to be able to get into the rooms to clean them. Even if you are going to have a small B&B, providing locks for the rooms (other than the simple slide bolt) is an amenity that means a lot to certain travelers, particularly first-time B&Bers.

Towel Valets

If the bathroom is shared, you'll need a standing towel rack of some sort in each guest room.

Fans

If you don't have air conditioning, you may want to supply each guest room with a good electric fan, either the oscillating type or a window fan. These should be in good working condition with a secure, safe cord.

The Extras

All of the above items are necessary from the start. There are, however, other amenities that you may add to your guest rooms after you've been in business awhile, such as:

Reading Chairs, Sofa, or Loveseat

If there is room, have a reading chair or loveseat in the room so that guests don't have to sit on the bed. Even a straight-backed chair next to the dresser is helpful. If you do add this furniture to the room, supply the sitting area with a reading lamp and small table.

Reading Materials

It's nice to keep a few current magazines and books in the guest rooms. Short story collections, novels, nonfiction, and any history about your area all make good reading for the traveler. A small bookcase can provide not only storage for reading materials but a spot for interesting (and not too valuable) objets d'art. If you don't have room for a bookcase, keep the magazines in an attractive basket and place a few books on one of the bedside tables.

Writing Table

If you have large-enough guest rooms, it is a very nice touch to supply each with a small writing table or desk. You may even stock the desk with a few of your own postcards, stamped, if you have some printed when you purchase brochures and business cards. Even something as simple as a metal French café table with two chairs is sufficient (these are commonly available in mail order catalogues); this addition can serve as a place to write postcards, refer to a road map when planning the next leg of a journey, or have early morning coffee, if you are going to offer this kind of room service.

Art

When you are able to add artwork to your rooms, the light touch is best. Collect work from local artists whenever possible: watercolors and etchings of your area will be appropriate and of interest to your guests. Old maps of your state or county, or new ones with notations on all historical points of interest, are also good additions to the walls. Your local newspaper may be able to provide you with enlargements of interesting old photos of your town in times past, and these can add a lovely as well as informative bit of interest to the rooms.

Television or Radio

Before you supply your guest rooms with radio and TV, ask yourself if the noise could be an annoyance to other guests. If your guest rooms share common walls and are not well insulated, consider the problems it could create for a couple trying to get to sleep or simply to read in bed, while a late-night show blasts away in the next room. Most B&B travelers don't expect TV in the room, and you can always have a living room for guests supplied with one. If you are able to conveniently offer TV in the guest rooms, you will have an amenity important to many Americans.

Telephones

There must be a phone available to guests in one of the common rooms, but there is no need to place them in the bedrooms. The exceptions are B&Bs located in major cities where the main source of bookings is the business traveler. These B&Bs may wish to offer this amenity to compete with hotels. If you are going to have phones in the rooms, the phone company will help you set up a system that allows only local calls to be placed from those phones. Any kind of long-distance call will be stopped by a block and the caller will have to use a credit card or reverse the charges in order to place the call. One phone line for every five guest rooms is considered sufficient; if your B&B has eight rooms, you'll need two phone lines for the guest room phones plus your own business line, making a total of three separate phone lines. This is obviously an added expense, but a necessity for most business travelers and one that will enable you to charge higher rates.

Suites

Being able to offer suites gives you an advantage as a B&B proprietor. A suite should include a bedroom, bathroom, and sitting room. Since a suite provides the guest with more space, you can charge more for a suite, even if what you did to create it was attach one bedroom to another, making a too-small bedroom into a charming sitting room. And if the sitting room is furnished with a daybed, convertible couch, or loveseat, this space can become a bedroom for children, allowing you to advertise a family suite. Parents of young children usually prefer that the children stay in the same room with them, but most bedrooms aren't large enough for a queen-sized bed and two rollaways. If you do plan to take families with children, setting aside a family suite helps ensure that young kids who want to watch TV or play with Legos won't be disturbing your other guests using the living room to read or chat.

Don'ts

As someone who has stayed at bed-and-breakfasts, you have seen first-hand what makes for a pleasing guest room and what does not. Keep these observations in mind as you set up your own guest rooms; personal experience is the best teacher.

I do think it's worthwhile to mention some of the emphatic *don'ts* that you should keep in mind as you set up your guest rooms. Here are some of the horror stories about B&B rooms that I've heard over the years or have experienced firsthand:

- a bedroom with no door, just a blanket hanging from a rod covering the doorway

- a bedroom with a curtain on a rod covering one corner of a bedroom, behind which were the sink and toilet of the "private bath"
- a bedroom with a camp-style portable toilet in the closet

Less horrific but still not satisfactory are examples that include extremely old and lumpy mattresses, bedspreads with stains and tears, closets with no hangers, doors with no locks, a bedroom still filled with the clothing and other personal belongings of an away-at-college child, a bedroom on a different floor from the bathroom, windows with no shades or curtains, paper-thin walls that allowed for no sense of privacy, and less-than-clean conditions in the room overall.

Spend a night in each of your guest rooms. That's the best way to find out what's right and what's wrong about them.

The Elements of Style

As you acquire all the basics for your guest rooms, you will be establishing a certain style. Many of my guests have asked me if I hired a decorator for my rooms (I did not) and want to know how I knew what to choose. It's quite simple, really. The age and style of your house will dictate, to a certain degree, the decor of the guest bedrooms. For instance, contemporary Scandinavian furniture would be out of place in a turn-of-the-century Victorian, as would southwestern style furniture in a Maine farmhouse. By complementing the style of the house with appropriate furnishings that you like, you will automatically be achieving a pleasing and unique environment. When I say "furnishings that you like," I mean to remind you that you needn't be a slave to a certain period of fashion. Just because your dream house is of the Victorian era, you don't have to go with a tufted sofa, lace doilies, ball-and-claw feet, and heavy window treatments—unless you want to. Choose antiques and pieces from various periods that you like and that complement the house. The result will be unique, lovely, and special—and very unlike any chain lodging!

When choosing colors for your guest rooms, keep in mind that lighter colors make a room seem larger and darker colors make one seem smaller. Also, certain vivid, dark colors may be in vogue this year, but once out of style will quickly make your rooms look dated. Pale classic colors are pleasing to the eye and are less likely to look out of date. As H. Jackson Brown, Jr., so aptly puts it in *Life's Little Instruction Book,* "When undecided about what color to paint a room, choose antique white."

You will quickly find (if you have not figured it out already) that preparing a guest room for B&B use is expensive. There are a number of things you can do to keep the initial cost down, however. Then you can allow the business to help pay for future improvements to the rooms.

The Frugal Decorator

For instance, it is much less expensive to paint a room than to wallpaper it. Paint costs less than wallpaper, and so does the labor to apply it, if you are hiring someone else to do the work. Wallpaper can be added later if that's the look you want for your rooms, but a freshly painted room, nicely furnished, can be quite satisfactory in the meantime. When I first opened my bed-and-breakfast, I didn't want to put too much money into the guest rooms—partly because we had other, more pressing things to spend it on, and partly because I wasn't sure I'd like running a B&B. So I started by giving the guest rooms a thorough cleaning and a fresh coat of paint. The rooms looked fine; although rather plain, they were certainly nice enough to stay in, and I kept my rates low. Over the next few years I added wallpaper and wallpaper borders, repainted the woodwork, installed new light fixtures, and refinished the antique hardware on the doors; new dust ruffles, comforters, pillow shams, and curtains were all added over time. If your guests can see that you are in the process of fixing up your house, room by room—and the rooms are clean and the rates are low—they will be willing to overlook any deficiency in the decor.

Yard sales and secondhand shops can be the source of many great and inexpensive finds for your B&B. You needn't purchase all your furniture at antique shops! Sign up for a refinishing or upholstering class at your local community center; this can be a good way to learn a new money-saving skill and to spread the word about your bed-and-breakfast business.

Another way to keep the cost down while preparing your rooms for business is to barter. Perhaps you can barter a stay at your B&B in return for some painting, wallpapering, stenciling, and the like. Or if you are in another business, such as catering, you can barter those goods or services in return for others. I know a host who bartered in this manner for stenciling and custom draperies. She ended up with spectacular-looking results, which she never could have afforded to pay for in cash. If you are going to try bartering, make your agreement a written one and be very specific. Your end of the agreement should only be due *after* the work is satisfactorily completed.

Cleanliness Is Next to Godliness

As you furnish and decorate each guest room, ask yourself how easy it will be to keep the room clean. A clean room is extremely important to the traveler. Although you will have to keep the entire house clean and tidy— at least the part which is visible and used by guests—their bedrooms are usually the most important rooms to guests and the places where they'll spend the most time. Limit the number of knickknacks, which just collect dust and are hard to clean. Doll collections, dried flower arrangements, antique hat collections, and the like are fun to look at but may be too much trouble for you or your helper to keep clean.

Housekeeping

What is a good standard of "clean"? The room should appear as if no one has ever stayed there before. On a daily basis while the room is occupied, with no change of guests, you will need to empty the wastebasket; make the bed; replace used towels with fresh ones; and if needed, dust and vacuum. For guests who have reserved an extended stay, sheets should be changed every third day.

When there is a change of guests, you will need to strip and remake the bed; dust and vacuum the room, including the closet, drawers, and any upholstered furniture; clean the mirror; clean the wastebasket; if necessary, wash the floor. Dusting includes all surfaces—baseboards, window sills, bookshelves, lampshades, etc. Check switchplates and doors for fingerprints that may need to be washed off. Be sure to check under the bed and in all drawers to see if guests left anything behind; if so, put the item aside to be mailed to their home.

If you are going to have hired help clean the rooms, you will have to train them. You should provide them with a checklist to follow, and you should still inspect the rooms regularly.

To make cleaning an easier task for you or for anyone working for you, set aside a closet for storing all the cleaning supplies used on a regular basis—the vacuum cleaner, vacuum cleaner bags, dust rags, polish, wood cleaner, glass cleaner and paper towels, dry and sponge mops, bucket with sponges, rubber gloves, toilet bowl brush, and cleansers for the bathroom. You will become a much more efficient cleaner, and a happier one, if you have all the tools needed neatly stored in one spot. If your B&B is very large, you'll want a storage closet like this on each floor. This is also a good place to keep the cleaning checklist for your helpers. One of the biggest bugaboos for B&B travelers are rooms that aren't clean enough. There should be no reason for a guest to have this complaint about your bed-and-breakfast.

Sweet Dreams

Other guest bedroom issues to consider are accessibility to the bathroom and to emergency exits. As you know, private baths for each guest room are the ideal, but shared or private, the bathroom should be easily accessible to the bedroom. And guest rooms on the second floor and higher should have some kind of emergency exit in the event of fire (more about this in chapter 7).

In addition to visiting other B&Bs for ideas on the perfect guest room, thumb through *Country Inns/Bed & Breakfast* magazine. You'll find some wonderful examples to inspire you. Don't be intimidated by the more elegant accommodations; each B&B is unique and your rooms should reflect your own good taste and style, not anyone else's. Put some love, care, and thought into each of your guest rooms, and you will have all the ingredients for the well-appointed guest room.

4

The Bed-and-Breakfast Bathroom

I have had a good many more
uplifting thoughts, creative and
expansive visions—while soaking
in comfortable baths or drying myself after bracing showers—in well-
equipped American bathrooms than
I have ever had in any cathedral.
—EDMUND WILSON

The Well-Appointed Guest Bath
(or The Hidden B in Bed-and-Breakfast)

*O*nce you're in business, you'll find the first or second question a prospective guest asks when calling to inquire about reservations is whether the
bath is private. Being able to offer private baths is ideal in this business;
you'll be able to charge higher rates than B&Bs with shared baths, and you
won't lose potential guests on that particular issue. And you can be assured
that guests who would otherwise find your B&B charming won't have
their stay spoiled by sharing a bath with some less-than-considerate
guests.

Years ago, when bed-and-breakfast lodging was still catching on in this
country, most small B&Bs offered shared baths, and B&B enthusiasts,
introduced to this form of lodging while traveling in England or Ireland,
expected to share a bath. Sharing a bath was part of the "roughing it"
aspect of B&B travel that this adventuresome crowd accepted in return for
the other extras—huge breakfasts, charming and out-of-the-ordinary locations, and low rates. That has changed, however, and nowadays travelers
expect a private bath. As B&Bs have become more popular and travelers

more discerning, the standards have become higher and more sophisticated. Today a polished B&B offers a private bath for each guest room.

You'll therefore want to pay attention to the number and location of bathrooms in a house—and the potential to add more—if you are shopping for a house to run as a B&B. If you have found your dream house and it does not include sufficient bathrooms, or if you are considering using your current house and would not be able to offer private baths, don't let that prevent you from opening a B&B. There are ways to make a shared bath arrangement work, at least temporarily, until you are able to add more full or half baths to the house.

Starting a B&B with Shared Bath

If you must start out with a shared bath, there are some do's and don'ts to consider. Do *not*, under any circumstances, plan on sharing your family bathroom with guests. You simply cannot reasonably keep a family bath clean enough for B&B standards, and you will greatly accelerate the likelihood of burnout if you are always trying to hustle out of your bathroom so that guests can use it. Your family bath will be home to your toiletries, medicines, and towels—a guest bath should never contain any of these items—and you will not want to find another place for them. Where would you keep these items? Your bedroom? Think again!

A shared bath should be used by guests *only,* and should not be shared by more than two rooms, whether double- or single-occupancy. It must contain all the elements in the following list, essential to any guest bath, shared or private, but it needs a few things as well that the private bath does not.

Manners, Please

First off, you will need to place a small, attractive sign in a shared guest bath (much like the house rules sign in each bedroom) reminding guests of a few courtesies. You can post it in a picture frame set on the sink vanity or on the table next to a pedestal sink, or on the inside of the door. Wherever you put it, the sign should be easily visible, pretty, and politely worded. Here are a few of the things you might want to include:

Bathroom Etiquette

This is a shared bath (unless you are the only guests in the house). Please observe these courtesies to make sharing the bath a more agreeable experience for all. Thank you!

- Please use the fan when showering or bathing.
- For your safety, always use the rubber mat when showering or bathing, and please hang it back up when you're done.
- Please do not leave personal toiletry items in the bathroom.
- Please do not leave your towels in the bathroom. Use the towel valets in your room.
- There is an outlet next to the mirror in your bedroom for your hair dryer.
- If you are sharing this bath with other guests, please be considerate of their needs too.
- Remember, there is a half bath for your use on the first floor.

Although you may think that the information given in this list of shared bath do's and don'ts is all pretty elementary, it is a good idea to remind guests of what you consider good etiquette in a shared bath situation. The sign will reassure those guests who are a bit nervous about sharing a bath, and it just may inspire some travelers to be a bit more considerate of their fellow guests. That said, however, you will find that some guests are extremely inconsiderate about how they use a shared bath, leaving behind piles of wet towels in a steam-filled room, toothpaste residue in the sink, and masses of hair clogging the shower drain. There is not much you can do about this, other than giving the room a complete cleaning, but that isn't always a reasonable solution since you can't make a habit of checking on the guest bath after each use! You'll usually be cleaning this room only once a day, each morning. If you happen to find the bathroom in this condition when you show it to new guests checking in, you'll have to ask them to give you a few minutes to tidy it up. Make a brief apology, then quickly do your best to make the room look as though no one else has used it.

You'll notice that the example of a bathroom etiquette list given here includes a note about a half bath on the first floor. Your house will probably have a half bath on the first floor, and if your guest baths are shared, you should make this half bath available to guests. Point it out to them when they first check in and you are showing them around. And if it is a bath used by your family, be sure family members understand that it must be kept clean and tidy because guests will be using it too. Even though it may not be on the same floor as their bedroom, guests will greatly appreciate having access to this bathroom.

Since you will be supplying the guest rooms that share a bath with towel valets, you'll need to keep some kind of hand towels in the shared bathroom; you can't expect guests to remember to carry their hand towels into the bathroom each time they use it. You can use the paper hand towels made for this purpose (pretty, but expensive); or you can keep a roll of paper towels in the bathroom, either on a paper towel holder or set in a pretty basket; or you can supply the bathroom with fresh linen hand towels every day, perhaps color-coordinated with the two guest rooms sharing the bath, making it clear to guests which hand towels are meant for whom.

For anyone wondering why the towels should be supplied on a towel valet in each guest room when the bath is shared, consider this: you won't have enough space to put all the bath towels for four adult guests in the bathroom. Even if you did, there would be someone who would use *all* the bath towels and leave them in a heap on the floor. Also, guests don't like the idea of anyone else using their towels—even to dry their fingertips! There are a variety of attractive towel valets (these are standing towel racks that look a lot like quilt racks) available at bath shops, department stores, and in mail order catalogues. See the appendix for resources.

Keep It Clean

The shared bath must be completely cleaned every day, including washing the floor, even when there is no change of guests. While the private bath must be tidied each day, it generally needs a complete cleaning only when there is a change of guests. In this regard, having shared guest baths makes more work for you, the host. Why be this picky? Because your guests won't be thrilled about the idea of sharing a bath (all travelers choose a private bath if given the choice), and the best way to make the arrangement more agreeable to them is to keep the bathroom spotlessly clean. Each morning, after your guests have had their breakfast and gone off for the day, you will need to empty the wastebasket; remove any towels; return any personal items to guest rooms (if you can identify where they belong); put a new roll of toilet paper on the holder; check the liquid soap dispenser at the sink; provide new hand towels, if needed; vacuum the room; scour the toilet, sink, and bath/shower; clean the mirror; replace the terry cloth mat with a fresh one; and wash the floor. When the floor is dry, put down a clean area rug. This routine will become second nature to you, but it is, as you can imagine, much more than you'll need to do daily in a private bath.

Semiprivate Baths

Some B&Bs advertise "semiprivate bath." What is meant by this, usually, is that each guest room has its own private half bath (sink and toilet) but that the bathroom with the tub and shower is shared. This arrangement is an improvement over a strictly shared bath, but the bath that is shared will still need to include all the elements and meet all the standards previously mentioned. If you are offering a semiprivate bath, it is acceptable for three guest rooms, rather than the normal maximum of two, to share the full bath.

Your B&B may end up having some rooms with private baths, some with semiprivate, and others with shared. This is fine because it will allow you to offer some rooms at a lower rate, and to certain travelers that is more important than a private bath. Families generally do not mind at all sharing a bath among themselves.

Adding Bathrooms to an Old House

Our house originally had seven bedrooms and one full bath! Today it would be unthinkable to build a house this way, but it's not unusual to find this kind of ratio in old houses. Fortunately, many of the old houses have alcoves, closets, and dressing rooms that can be nicely transformed into bathrooms, full or half. Often what were very small children's rooms are unsuitable as guest rooms for a B&B but are ideal as roomy, luxurious bathrooms.

Unless you're experienced with renovation, remodeling, and design, you'll probably want advice from a builder or architect on how best to add bathrooms to your house, old or new. A professional should be able to provide you with ideas that you never would have come up with on your own and that will be in keeping with the age and character of your house.

A word of caution: If you are adding bathrooms that will not have windows, it is of utmost importance that they have powerful ventilation. Small, windowless bathrooms are breeding grounds for mildew and can quickly become dank, unpleasant places. Be sure the builder knows you want the most powerful bathroom fan and vent available, and consider tying the ventilation switch to the light switch so that the fan is automatically turned on whenever the room is used. Sometimes when a window is not possible, a skylight is. It's worth the extra money to have it installed. It will add light and ventilation and make a small bathroom seem larger and more luxurious.

The Necessities

Whether your guest baths are shared, semiprivate, or private, they all need to be clean, bright, and attractive. This effect can be achieved in part by using the right materials in installing or remodeling. A bathroom with a window or skylight is always preferable to one with none. All bathrooms, as mentioned, should have powerful fan/ventilation systems. The fixtures should be of top quality—vitreous china for the sink and toilet, enameled cast iron for the tub. Avoid fiberglass if possible: it is harder to clean and doesn't last as long as porcelain, enamel, Corian (or other solid-surface materials), and ceramic tile. White fixtures will always be in style and always look fresh and clean. Ceramic tile floors are the best choice for bathrooms. They are easy to clean and long-lasting, and they lend a classic look to the room. There is an almost dizzying selection of colors and styles to choose from; select something that you'll be happy to live with a long time and something that complements the age of your house and decor of your guest rooms. Wall-to-wall carpeting is not appropriate for a bathroom: it will get wet and never dry out thoroughly, causing mildew, and it cannot be kept properly clean.

It goes without saying that a bathroom contains a sink and toilet. But even these basic items should be chosen with care. In addition to using good materials, consider the following list of details and items as necessities in the well-appointed guest bath:

Sink

The sink should have a large basin and a single spigot that mixes the hot and cold water. The charming but inconvenient double spigots found in the old sinks—all hot or all cold—are pretty but not practical. If you install a pedestal sink, there should be some kind of table or stand next to it for guests to use for storing their toiletries. If you choose a sink with a vanity counter, make sure it's high enough to be comfortable and that there is enough counter surface.

Mirror

There should be a large and well-lit mirror over the sink for your guests to use for shaving, applying makeup, and styling their hair. All too often, this simple necessity is not found in B&B baths: the mirror either is too small, does not have sufficient lighting, or both.

GFI Outlet

This stands for "ground fault interrupter"; any licensed electrician will know what it is. Today this kind of electrical outlet is required by building codes. It is a unit that contains an individual breaker that will trip the current if the appliance in use touches water, thereby preventing shock or electrocution in the bathroom. The outlet has a small button on it to press if the current is interrupted. The outlet should be near the sink and mirror and high enough off the floor that your guests could easily use it for their electric toothbrush, shaver, hair dryer, or electric curlers while standing up. The outlet should also be conveniently near the vanity counter or small table next to a pedestal sink so that guests have a place to set the appliances.

Toilet

The toilet seat should be in perfect condition, and there should not be any trick to flushing the toilet! I advise against using those ruglike toilet lid and tank covers; they are magnets for dirt and detract from an otherwise clean appearance in a bathroom. If you do use these, you are adding to your laundry chores.

Toilet Paper

It is not a good idea simply to have a roll of toilet paper sitting on the top of the tank. Many people will not find it convenient, and the roll can easily fall into the toilet. Instead, install an attractive, sturdy toilet paper holder. Buy white, unscented toilet paper, and have an extra supply of three rolls in an obvious spot in the bathroom.

Tub and Shower

The ideal combination in a guest bath is a five-foot tub that is also a shower, surrounded by a three-sided enclosure that is tiled or faced with Corian or another suitable material. Corian, while an expensive material, is not any more expensive than tile, especially when you figure in labor costs. It is good-looking, incredibly rugged, and easier to keep clean than tile and grout—an important consideration in this business. The tub should be enameled cast iron, not steel. Steel tubs are much less expensive, but they flex, chip, and rust. Or you may opt for the single-piece fiberglass tub/shower unit. Although they can be more difficult to keep clean, they offer an affordable alternative to tile or Corian and have the one advantage of being seamless.

Some bathrooms have only enough room for a shower stall. If that is the case in some of your baths, be sure the shower stall is the largest size possible (thirty-six inches is about as small as is comfortable) and of the best quality you can get. Fiberglass is an easy option; tiled or Corian walls in a custom-built shower are more expensive but may give better wear and be more attractive. The floor of the shower and tub should have a nonslip surface, as well as a rubber mat. Shower doors will keep the water in the shower stall better than a shower curtain. If you buy shower doors, get clear glass: it's easy to tell if they're clean. If you buy shower curtains, keep extra liners on hand, as you will have to replace these regularly. The shower stall should have a rack or shelf for soap and shampoo. Don't expect your guests to be happy keeping these items on the shower floor.

Older houses often have long, lovely claw-foot tubs and no showers. These are wonderful for bath lovers, but your average American is addicted to a daily shower. You can add a hand-held shower spray to a claw-foot tub, but many travelers will find this less than satisfactory. If you're going to keep the claw-foot tubs, consider adding the oval shower curtain bars designed for turning these old beauties into tub/showers. See the appendix for resources.

Good Water Pressure

There should be good water pressure at the sink, tub, and shower, and a more-than-sufficient supply of hot water. Be sure your plumber knows that all baths may be in use at the same time and that all will need adequate water pressure. You will probably want to have a larger hot water heater installed as well.

Smooth Walls and Ceilings

The walls and ceilings in your bathrooms should be smooth, not textured, and painted with gloss or semigloss paint to avoid mildew stains and make cleaning easier. Gloss paint will also add more light to the room than flat paint. If you decide to use wallpaper in the bathrooms, be sure it is of a quality to withstand all the steam and moisture it will be subjected to.

Good Lighting

There should be an overhead light in the bathroom, as well as lights flanking the bathroom mirror, and they should not be fluorescent. In addition, it's a nice touch to provide your guest baths with night lights.

Towel Bars

Whether the bath is shared or private, there should be an appropriate number of attractive, sturdy towel bars in the room. Even if the bath is shared and you have supplied the guest rooms with towel valets, your

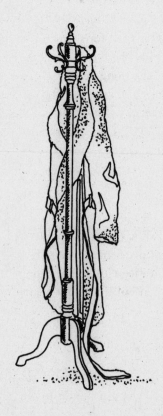

guests will want to be able to hang up their towels while they are shaving, brushing their teeth, or soaking in the tub. There should also be a hook on the back of the door for them to hang their clothes on.

Terry Cloth Bath Mat

A heavy terry cloth bath mat should be hanging on a bar next to the tub or shower. Replace it daily with a fresh one.

Small Rug

A small cotton rug, placed in front of the sink, gives your guests something a bit more pleasant to stand on while brushing their teeth than the cold, hard tile floor. It should be machine washable with a nonskid backing, and you'll need more than one so that you can replace it with a fresh one when needed.

Tissues

Even though there will be toilet paper in the bathroom, you should also provide a box of white, unscented tissues.

Drinking Cups

Guest baths should have disposable paper drinking cups. Glass is too dangerous, and plastic is too unsanitary. Paper cups are sold with fairly plain wall-mounted or shelf-style dispensers, which are perfectly suitable for any decor. Do not leave a stack of paper cups on the side of the sink. They won't be sanitary and they'll get in your guests' way. Some hosts provide a basket of disposable cups, but again, this arrangement is not as easy to use or as clean as a dispenser designed to hold the cups.

Wastebasket

Why does anyone forget to provide a bathroom with a wastebasket? This is an absolute necessity. Make it the sort that can be washed.

Room Freshener

A can of air freshener spray, placed where guests can easily spot it, is a thoughtful item, especially in a shared guest bath.

Window Treatment

If your bathrooms have windows, they should be fitted with a shade or blind that will provide complete privacy when closed. The curtain, if you use one, can be purely decorative.

Lock

The bathroom door should lock from the inside, assuring your guests complete privacy. A sliding bar lock is perfect for this purpose.

Soap

Keep a container of liquid hand soap, mild and perfume-free, at the sink. For the shower, you may provide a container of liquid bath soap, or one bar of hard soap per person. You can purchase the small, travel-sized bars from hotel and motel suppliers at pennies per bar. If you provide full-sized bars of soap, you'll be wasting money, since you'll need to supply fresh soap to each new guest. See the appendix for resources.

Towels

Bath towels are an important item to your guests. As with sheets, I recommend white towels, and for the same reasons: they are easy to match when you need to add to your supply, they can be bleached, and they always look fresh. You may want to use colors, and that's fine, but whatever you do, don't use a mishmash of your old towels in a faded rainbow of colors. The towels should be all-cotton, high-quality terry cloth, looped and fluffy on both sides; the velvet finish towels are not as absorbent. Provide each guest with a washcloth, hand towel, and two or three large bath towels per day. It is not necessary, or even a good idea, to provide guests with bath sheets. These are so large as to be awkward to use, and you'll only be able to fit two or three in your washer at a time. Two or three large bath towels per adult, replenished daily, is perfectly sufficient. Replace used towels daily. Whether you hang towels on bars or place them on a valet, fold them in thirds the long way, so that the bound edges face in, and then fold them in half twice.

These are the basic items you'll need to equip your guest baths, and you'll be doing just fine if you provide these and nothing more. There are, however, a few extras to consider adding; maybe you'd like guests to remember the luxurious baths when they think of your B&B. Indeed, this feature could become the hallmark of your bed-and-breakfast.

The Extras

As you may have found from your own experience, some B&Bs stock guest baths with thick terry robes for the guests to use while there. This can be a real treat, since most travelers won't bother to pack such a bulky item, even if they have one at home. These same B&Bs often offer Jacuzzi baths and an assortment of bubble baths, bath oils, and bath salts. The opportunity to relax in an oversized tub, soaking in a fragrant bubble bath, and later to lounge in a big cozy robe while reading a good book is a luxury most of us can't find the time for during our regular busy schedules. For the bath aficionado, these extras can make a B&B stay memorable.

If you plan on offering extras like these, you'll be able to mention them in your brochures and advertising, and you'll want to charge slightly higher rates than if you were not including these special items.

You Must Remember This

The final must for your guest baths is that they be spotlessly clean. I've already stressed how important cleanliness is when the bath is shared, but shared or private, your guests should get the impression they are the first ones ever to use that bathroom. If you will be having hired help cleaning the baths, be sure your helper follows your checklist carefully. Check on the work to make certain it's up to your standards. To make this chore a little easier for you or your helper, keep the cleaning supplies organized and in a tote or bucket, which can be kept in your cleaning supply closet or under a vanity-style sink.

A well-equipped bath, kept clean and fresh, will be as important to the success of your business as any other element, and will help ensure that your guests return again and again.

The Well-Equipped Bath

Bath Linens
to be replaced fresh daily:

1 terry cloth bath mat

2 large bath towels per person

1 hand towel per person

1 washcloth per person

If your B&B will accommodate a maximum of six guests a night, you will need to have *at least* three sets of towels and washcloths per person and three bath mats per bathroom for a minimum supply. As soon as your finances allow, you will be more secure doubling the number of bath linens.

Optional:

3 non-slip, washable area rugs per bathroom

5

Public Rooms in the
Bed~and~Breakfast

> *Do* you know that conversation is
> one of the greatest pleasures in life?
> But it wants leisure.
> —W. SOMERSET MAUGHAM

A Place for Guests

Although the name bed-and-breakfast might imply a pretty basic, bare-bones package—a room for the night and breakfast in the morning (and in years past this was the standard)—B&B travelers today expect to have the use of at least one other room in addition to their bedroom. As mentioned in chapter 2, the more common-use space you can make available to your guests (indoors and out), the better. Common areas will allow your guests a sense of expansive comfort while they are staying with you and will ensure you and your family true privacy in your own family room.

A Living Room of One's Own

You must, at the least, offer your guests the use of a living room. It should not be the same living room that you and your family use, especially if you will have children living at home. Although there will be frequent occasions when you join your guests in "their" living room—and these times spent chatting about world travels, great restaurants, must-see movies, other B&Bs, and the like can be some of the most enjoyable you'll spend as a host—there will also be plenty of evenings when all you want to do is kick your shoes off, put your feet up, and have a glass of wine in peace and solitude. If you don't have a separate family room for this kind of let-your-hair-down behavior, you'll be forced to retreat to your bedroom. Eventually you'll resent being forced out of your own living room by those strangers, your guests.

If you have children living at home, there will be evenings when they'll want to have friends over to watch a movie on television. Soon they'll be spilling popcorn, talking loudly, and generally being kids. If you only have one living room/TV room/family room in the house, this scenario will discourage your B&B guests from using the room—especially if they were looking forward to sitting down for a good read while their travel companion takes a nap. So for your own privacy and that of your guests, you and your family need your own separate space.

Another reason to have a separate family room is that the living room you make available to guests must be kept looking neat, clean, polished, and welcoming at all times. Take a look around your living room now. Is there a jacket thrown across the back of the couch; is there a stack of unopened mail on the coffee table; is there a dog asleep on the rug? Are you in the habit of dropping the laundry basket next to the couch so that you can fold towels while you watch the news, or do your running shoes never seem to make it back up to your bedroom closet after a workout? If the answer is yes to any of these questions, you should be able to see the other reason you'll need your own private living room. You'll be working very hard to keep your house and grounds up to B&B standards; leave yourself one room where you and your family can relax and be yourselves.

You may also have to change some of your habits, at least during the months that you're open for business, to avoid potentially embarrassing moments. For instance, if you are in the habit of stumbling down to your kitchen in your pajamas in the early morning, ask yourself how you'd feel if a guest were to see you this way. I'd never considered this until it happened to me one morning.

I like to get up early, but I don't get dressed or put in my contact lenses until I've had a cup of coffee. So I make my way down the stairs and to the kitchen with my eyes barely open (I know the way by heart) and push the button on the coffee maker.

One morning, as I was almost at the bottom of the stairs, I heard a deep voice coming from the living room say, "Good morning." It wasn't my husband, so I assumed it was a guest. But I didn't know who it was because I couldn't even see him (I'm very nearsighted), and if he hadn't spoken I wouldn't have known anyone was even in the room. But he could obviously see me, and much more of me than I would have liked; it was summer and I was wearing a short, lightweight nightgown. It was an awkward moment.

Now, even if I think it's too early for anyone else to be up, if there are guests in the house I put on my glasses and a robe before going downstairs. And when I close the B&B for the season, one of the little pleasures I revel in is going down for coffee wearing whatever I want, and without my glasses.

The Well-Appointed B&B Living Room

The living room that you provide for guests to use should be comfortably furnished and attractively decorated. It should contain one or more couches or loveseats; a coffee table; a couple of comfortable armchairs, with ottomans, if possible, and small side tables; and good reading lamps. These are, however, just the basics.

Some Extras

If the room is large enough, you might want to include a writing desk (stocked with stamped postcards of your B&B). Your guests will appreciate this thoughtful extra and may end up doing a little nearly free advertising for you in the process. If you aren't going to supply each guest bedroom with a television, then you should have one in this room, hidden in a cabinet if possible so as not to detract from the beauty of the room. This may also be the room where you provide a phone for guests: they will need to make dinner reservations, call home, and call the friends or relatives whom they came to town to visit. The phone should be on a table with a pad and pencil, and there should be a comfortable chair next to the phone table. If you provide a cordless phone for guests, they have the option of carrying the phone to another area for privacy or to get away from the noise in the living room. (By the way, I've never yet had any guest abuse telephone privileges. They use phone cards or call collect when making long-distance calls.) If there is a radio in the living room that you want your guests to know about, be sure to point it out to them when you show them around. You might keep the receiver set on a reliable classical music station. There should be some reading material in the living room; it's a thoughtful touch to place a daily newspaper on the coffee table, along with current magazines. Some B&Bs, especially the ones that cater to families with young children, will provide a chest of board games in this room or simply leave a checkerboard set up at a small table for two. If you have a piano that no one in your family plays and there's room for it in the guests' living room, by all means put it in there. Every now and then a talented player will delight you and your guests with an impromptu concert.

The Beauty Part

It need not be extravagant, but the room should have aesthetic appeal, and the style you set will be a reflection of you. All of the furnishings should be in very good condition; don't get a new couch for your family room and put the old, worn one in the B&B parlor! Always go for the highest-quality upholstery fabrics you can afford. These will wear best and will lend a substantial air of comfort to the room. Or instead of upholstery, consider slipcovers, which are easy to clean, for the couches and chairs. You could have two sets—one for summer, one for winter. Then, if you're open for business year-round, guests who stay with you during both seasons can enjoy the change in ambiance. You could do the same with the draperies (one set for winter, one for summer) and create two distinct moods for the same room.

Plants add a nice touch, as do bookshelves, local artwork, and cut flowers. The room should be kept clean and tidy—pillows plumped and tables gleaming. Don't forget to leave a stack of coasters in an obvious place.

If the room offers an inviting view, expect your guests to want to spend some time there and arrange the furniture accordingly. Windows should be sparkling clean and should open and close easily. They should be fitted with some kind of drapery, shade, or shutter that can be closed in the evening for privacy.

If the living room has a fireplace, either keep a fire lit for guests during cool weather or leave the kindling, logs, and matches available for guests to build a fire themselves. The fireplace *must* have a screen, and guests should be told that it is always to be in place when the fireplace is in use.

Room for a Crowd

Any or all of these elements will make your B&B living room a very nice place indeed and will be well appreciated by your guests. If you are going to have a small operation, one such living room is sufficient, although even for a small B&B, more than one common room is a plus. If you are going to have a large operation, it's almost a necessity to have more than one common room for guests, as the previous description of elements may have suggested to you. For one thing, a B&B with six or more guest rooms will have twelve or more guests in the house at one time during full occupancy. One living room will quickly start to seem crowded and insufficient. If you have two living rooms for guests, one can have a TV and the other can be for reading and socializing; some people find television to be an unpleasant intrusion, while others can't call it a day without an hour or so of TV.

Many of the large old American houses had two living rooms or parlors—one for formal occasions and one for everyday use (much as newer homes now have a living room and a family room). If this is the case in the house you plan to use for your bed-and-breakfast, consider reserving both parlors for guests only, and look into adding on a family room off the kitchen for you and your family.

In addition to a living room for guests, your house may have a sun room or library that you'll be making available to them. These rooms can be especially inviting. Imagine your guests' delight to find that they can enjoy their first cup of coffee and the morning paper in the sun room before breakfast, or that afternoon tea is available there at 4:00 P.M. To add a special extra, how about sherry in the library each evening before the dinner hour? There are many special little amenities you can add to your B&B that will make your guests feel pampered, and any of these will help create wonderful memories of their stay with you. These extras can be especially important if your house or location are not particularly remarkable; they can set your B&B apart from others in the area.

At Ease in a New Place

All of these common rooms should appear inviting. They should beckon to the guest to sit down and read for a while or to chat with other guests. You'll want to avoid anything that says "don't touch," such as clear plastic slipcovers over the furniture (yes, I've been asked if this would be a good idea for a B&B), or a cramped seating arrangement that says "no one ever really uses this room." The more at ease guests feel in your house, and the more of it they know they have access to (whether they use all the rooms or not), the more likely it is that they will return again and again.

The Great Outdoors

Don't limit yourself to providing extra space for your B&B guests inside your house; outdoor "rooms" such as porches, decks, and patios can be wonderful places to while away an hour or two. You may not think your porch is anything special, but to your guests from an upper-story apartment in a large city, it's a little bit of paradise. Even if the view is of nothing more than your neighborhood and the street, a comfortably furnished porch bedecked with lush plants becomes another appealing spot for the road-weary traveler to stop, relax, and reflect on the day. And don't forget, the view may have become quite mundane to you, but your guests will be seeing it with new eyes, and to them there is bound to be *something* of interest! Furnish your porch appropriately: there is handsome wicker, metal, and wooden porch furniture available nowadays. You'll want to have tables as well as chairs and benches, and rocking chairs and porches were meant for each other. Old-fashioned gliders have come back in fashion, and if your porch is large enough, one of these can be an inviting addition. Hanging baskets of flowering plants can help make the porch seem like more of a room and add fragrance as well. Or perhaps a lattice screen covered with climbing roses or wisteria is more appropriate for your setting. During the warm weather, you'll find your porch is used as often or more than the living room you provide for guests.

A porch or deck, though outside, is still part of the house. A patio, on the other hand, allows your guests to have some kind of yard to use. If your

yard is large enough, consider creating a private area for guests. The patio can be brick or fieldstone and, depending on size, could have one or two umbrella tables, café furniture, chaises, or simply rustic benches. It can be edged with a bit of lawn or surrounded by flower beds; it can be cool and shaded or open to full sun all day. A close or distant view of hills, water, or even a bird feeder can give the area a focal point. Fencing, a clipped hedge, or shrubs can provide privacy from the part of the yard you reserve for family use. You may have a large property that you want to make entirely available to guests: this could well be one of the selling points of your B&B. Ponds, rose gardens, arbors, and gazebos are all possibilities, and many B&Bs offer guests use of tennis courts and pools. (This will, of course, increase your liability and insurance premium; more about that in chapter 7.) These special extras will make your B&B even more of haven, and if you want to cater to wedding parties, you could even allow receptions on the grounds, for an extra fee, of course.

Your Own Piece of Paradise

There are reasons *not* to make your entire yard available to your guests, as you may have already guessed. Just as you will need your own private living or family room, you may need to keep part of your yard private. If you now find that spending an hour alone in the garden is the perfect way to escape the stresses of the day, by all means keep a portion of it solely for your use. If you have a dog that is confined to your back yard, this is certainly a reason to restrict guests from it. Even the best of dogs have been known to get into trouble with strangers, and your guests may accidentally let the dog out of the yard. You may have a lovely pool that is *the* spot for your kids and their friends all summer; don't expect them to give it up once you start running a B&B, and don't expect your guests to find the "yard with pool" you advertised up to their expectations when they discover it's the private realm of in-residence adolescents.

Other Extras

Some B&Bs advertise a yard with use of a grill. This is a generous extra; if it's a charcoal grill, be prepared to supply guests with charcoal and lighter fluid. Guests will also need to use your refrigerator to store the hamburger meat, chicken, hot dogs, and so on until they are ready to cook them, and you will undoubtedly be asked to "loan" condiments—ketchup, relish, mustard, and the like. Guests will need to use your grilling tools, and unless they remembered paper plates and plastic cutlery, they will be asking you for these too. When they're done, there will be trash to clean up. And you probably won't feel comfortable leaving the house knowing that unfamiliar guests have a fire going in your back yard, so you'll be that much more restricted in your comings and goings. If you really want to offer this extra, however, consider packaging up paper plates, plastic cutlery, and little packets of condiments in a quantity to serve a family of four and keeping these on hand to sell at a reasonable price to the guests who want to grill but forget to bring everything but the meat. If possible, have an extra refrigerator in the garage or garden shed that is just for guests' use. Supply the grilling area with picnic tables and trash bins, and if you want guests to separate items for recycling, be sure to tell them and to label the bins. If you've prepared yourself ahead of time, offering this extra—outdoor grilling and dining—will mean a lot to certain guests, especially city dwellers and families with young children, and may just be the reason they return year after year.

It is more common to find B&Bs with substantial grounds encouraging guests to "spread a picnic blanket under one of our apple trees and enjoy an alfresco meal put together by one of our local gourmet markets," and this is also a great advertising draw. If you do this, be sure to have menus

and phone numbers readily available for guests, as well as directions and information on which shops deliver.

A Place for Smokers

Smoke-free public places are becoming the law in many towns and cities and certainly the trend in most businesses. Unless you smoke, and even if you do, you should not allow smoking in your B&B except for certain areas. It makes sense for these areas to be outside—on your porch, deck, or patio—so that the smoke doesn't bother other guests and the chance of a fire due to careless smoking is minimized. Smoking is another reason to have at least one outside area for guests, and if you do allow smoking there, be sure to supply a table or two with ashtrays. Empty the ashtrays on a regular basis; check them each morning and in the evening before going to bed. You won't need to (and shouldn't) leave matches with the ashtrays: smokers have their own or carry lighters.

Meeting the Special Needs of Business Travelers

If your bed-and-breakfast will be catering mostly to business travelers, the living room you provide may become a place for your business guests to rendezvous with clients before going out to dinner or off to a meeting. Large B&Bs that are heavily used by business travelers often have, in addition to living rooms, a conference room equipped with a long table and chairs, screen and projector, easels, and other supplies needed by business persons. These B&Bs also offer a phone in each guest room (as mentioned in chapter 3), as well as television. They usually have a fax machine available in one of the common rooms. But even the business traveler appreciates access to a green area and the other extras mentioned in this chapter, and these amenities may bring them back again for vacations with their families.

My House Is Your House

When you're staying at other B&Bs, make a mental note about what common rooms and areas were available and what features you found most appealing. Then incorporate some of these ideas into your own B&B. You may not be able to do as much as your favorite B&B, but as long as you include some of the elements mentioned in this chapter, you will be on the right track. Remember, what you are trying to do is to provide your guests with something more than just a room and a breakfast. With that in mind, set up your house as a haven, not just for you and your family but for another set of people too—your guests. You'll almost be planning two houses in one, but you'll want the house to present a seamless appearance, at least to your guests, so that they sense the house is really theirs, temporarily. If you make the effort and plan carefully, you will undoubtedly succeed in making your house a home sweet home for you and a home away from home for the weary and grateful traveler.

6

Breakfast

*L*ife, within doors, has few
pleasanter prospects than a neatly
arranged and well-provisioned
breakfast table.
—NATHANIEL HAWTHORNE

Wake Up and Smell the Coffee

*B*reakfast at a bed-and-breakfast *should* be special and usually is, as you no doubt know from your own travels. In fact, the memories of those wonderful breakfasts may actually be a large part of the reason you are starting your own B&B. Those were times when you shared travel stories with other guests, learned more about your host, and enjoyed a delicious meal served to you in delightful surroundings. The fact that this wonderful extra is included in the price of the lodging—not the case at hotels, and motels don't have dining rooms—makes B&Bs even more of a treat.

One of the reasons bed-and-breakfasts have become so popular is the reputation they've acquired for serving splendid and out-of-the-ordinary breakfasts in a fashion that makes guests feel truly pampered. Americans are starved for real home-cooked food, not to mention caring service, and are astonished and delighted to be invited to enjoy a leisurely breakfast at a carefully set and well-laden table. The muffins they're enjoying were made fresh that morning, and there is *real* butter on the table. Preserves are homemade, coffee beans are ground just before the pot is brewed, and the table is beautifully set. All the while, guests are attended to and served by someone who truly cares. But many B&B hosts go beyond these rather simple touches, especially the ones who serve a full breakfast.

Breakfast Options

Should you serve a full breakfast or the lighter (and easier) continental fare? Should you serve it buffet-style or family-style, or will you serve your guests at a set time? There are advantages and disadvantages to all of these options; you will have to decide for yourself what works best for you. Your decision will be based, in part, on whether or not you like to cook, how well and quickly you cook, how much time you'll have in the morning before going off to another commitment, and whether or not you have a preference for one or the other as a traveler yourself. (Another factor that could affect your decision is whether the zoning in your area restricts you to a continental breakfast only, as is the case in some places.) Whatever kind of breakfast fare you decide to offer, make it something special. This is your time to shine. Attention to small details can make even a continental breakfast memorable—freshly squeezed juice, homemade baked goods warm from the oven, and a table that's downright pretty. These little extras, combined with your caring, attentive service, are the ingredients for success.

Let's start with some definitions. A continental breakfast consists of coffee or tea and a roll or muffin. Add to that some juice, fresh fruit, yogurts, and various cereals and you have what's known as a continental-plus. A full breakfast can include all of the above but will also offer a main dish like pancakes and sausage, or bacon and eggs. These meals can be very basic or quite fancy, including such dishes as fruit-filled French toast, eggs Florentine, sausage casseroles, and elegant strudels, which lead some B&Bs to call their full breakfasts "gourmet." Brunch is a cross between a full breakfast and lunch, and is usually served later than breakfast. In addition to the items you'd expect to find at a full breakfast, brunch can include quiches, glazed ham, various vegetable dishes, more than one breakfast pastry, and even a dessert. It is most often served buffet-style so that guests may choose from a variety of dishes, and B&Bs that serve a true brunch usually do so only on Sundays.

If you serve a full breakfast, you can charge higher rates than B&Bs in your area that do not. Although business restrictions in most regions will specify that you are charging for the room *only*—breakfast at a B&B is considered an amenity included in the price of the room—it only makes sense that the more you are offering, the higher your rates will be. Also, many travelers are looking specifically for B&Bs that serve a full breakfast, so if you do, you'll be attracting more business and not losing any prospective guests on this issue. If your breakfasts are really something outstanding, your reputation may be built (and quickly) on that one item—an important point to consider, especially if your guest rooms are nice but not knockouts.

Some B&Bs offer a continental breakfast on weekdays and a full breakfast on weekends, or a pull-out-all-the-stops brunch on Sundays. The rates are slightly lower during the week, as you might guess, and higher on weekends. This setup works well for most travelers and is great for a host who enjoys cooking for a crowd, but not seven days a week. And many Americans are perfectly happy with continental fare during the week but look forward to a special breakfast on weekends. This setup might work well for you. Perhaps you love to bake, but aren't an expert with eggs Benedict; if so, consider starting your business with this kind of weekday/weekend alternate breakfast offering. Then, after a few months in business, you'll be able to decide whether you want to stay with this plan or switch exclusively to one of the two. Once you've been a host for a while, you'll know how important the breakfast is to *your* guests, and you'll know if you really have what it takes to cook and serve a full breakfast every day of the week.

When to Serve

You'll need to set specific times for breakfast, whether you serve a full or continental, and this information should be mentioned to guests when they check in, as well as posted somewhere in the guest rooms. That way your guests know when to plan on getting up, and you know, for instance, when to put the muffins in the oven. You don't want to serve muffins that came out of the oven an hour and a half earlier!

When your guests check in, show them around the house and point out the dining room or wherever you will be serving breakfast, and explain when breakfast is available. If you'll have more than one seating and it's a full breakfast, ask them which seating they'd prefer. This is also a good time to ask if your guests have any dietary restrictions that you should know about, such as vegetarian, low-salt, etc. You might also ask if guests have any special breakfast favorites and if they prefer coffee or tea in the morning. The better prepared you are to serve your guests the next morning, the happier they will be.

Don't tell your guests that breakfast is whenever they want it. You will lose any semblance of a schedule trying to accommodate guests who want to eat as early as 7:00 A.M. and as late as 11:00. If this doesn't sound like a problem to you now, believe me, it will once you're in business!

If you offer a full breakfast with only one serving time, make sure your dining room table is large enough to seat all your guests at once. One seating makes your morning schedule much easier—you know exactly when to start cooking, when to put things in the oven, and when to start a fresh pot of coffee—as well as shortening the time you have to spend in the kitchen each morning. However, offering breakfast at only one seating is a bit restrictive, and some guests will find this a reason not to return to your B&B. It's really just as easy to offer two seatings, as long as you find out from your guests in advance which one they'd prefer. To help determine when those seatings should be, find out from other hosts in your area when they serve breakfast. (I have found that the majority of B&B guests want breakfast between 8:30 and 9:30, and this is what I hear from other hosts as well.) Start your first season in business with options for when breakfast may be had that you think will be most agreeable to your guests and to you. Stay flexible, and be prepared to change those hours later if necessary to what actually works best.

If your rooms will be sharing a bath, it is unrealistic, and unfair to guests, to offer only one breakfast sitting. You can imagine the traffic jam in the morning when two couples who don't know one another have to share a bath and try to get to the dining room for one seating.

A full breakfast will generally require an hour to prepare, guests usually spend an hour at the breakfast table, and cleanup afterwards takes about an hour. As you can see, you will have to set some limits or you will never have enough time to do all the other things that need to be done to keep a B&B running.

If you are going to offer a continental breakfast, you can be much more flexible about when it's available, since quite often a continental breakfast is a self-serve affair. But even if it isn't going to be a buffet, a continental breakfast requires so much less preparation time than a full breakfast that you can afford to give your guests longer breakfast hours. If you decide to offer a buffet continental breakfast, let your guests know what hours breakfast will be available, say between 8:00 and 10:00 A.M. and set everything out for them just a few minutes before the earliest seating. If you have a small B&B, you should be able to set out a thermal carafe of coffee, cream and sugar, a basket of muffins, butter and jams, a pitcher of juice, and so on, and then be free to go about your business for the morning. If yours is a larger operation, you'll need to be on hand to replenish the coffee with a fresh pot, at the very least. Either way, you or a helper should be within earshot of guests during breakfast in case anyone needs something.

If your breakfast is a buffet, some things should be on ice and some on warming trays. You may want to have on the sideboard a commercial coffee maker that includes a pot of hot water for tea. Be sure to provide tea bags—regular and herbal—as well as milk for the tea (you will have cream for coffee) and lemon wedges. Since you won't be serving guests, you'll want to anticipate any and all requests in advance.

It's a nice touch to have coffee or tea available for your guests earlier than the breakfast hour. Some B&Bs will place a coffee tray outside the guest room doors at a prearranged time or will simply tell guests that they can help themselves in the dining room (or sun room, or whatever the case may be) from 7:00 A.M. on, or as early as you are prepared to hear and see guests milling about.

Business travelers like to eat breakfast early, and if you are going to cater mostly to that crowd, be prepared to have a breakfast—full or continental—ready as early as 7:00 A.M. Other B&B travelers who generally like an early breakfast are winter skiers, birders, and sport fishermen, to name a few, so if your business will be attracting any of these in sizable numbers, you must be prepared to serve an early breakfast, as well as a later breakfast to guests who do not need (or want!) to be up at the crack of dawn. Business travelers are usually content with a lighter breakfast, but most of these other early risers will want a full breakfast. You will be able to succeed in this business by offering either full or continental breakfasts—as long as you do it *well*.

Where to Serve Breakfast

If you have a beautiful dining room, by all means use it for breakfast. So many Americans have dining rooms but never use them, instead eating in the kitchen or family room while watching TV, that it will be a treat for most of your guests to be offered breakfast in a more elegant setting. Don't feel limited to this one room, however, especially if your house also has an inviting porch, a patio, or a sunny country kitchen. Where you decide to serve breakfast will depend on the style of your house, your location, and the kind of guests you are hoping to attract. If your B&B is in California wine country, for instance, expect guests to want to have the option of eating breakfast outdoors on a patio. If your house is a ski lodge, perhaps a rustic pine table in front of a roaring fire in the great room is more appropriate. A bed-and-breakfast in New England could entice guests with breakfast at umbrella tables in the garden during the summer months. As you'll discover when you visit other B&Bs, breakfast may be served just about anywhere, and part of being a good host is figuring out where that should be in *your* B&B.

Many B&B hosts offer breakfast in their kitchens. If you are considering doing this, be sure that your kitchen is roomy enough, and clean and tidy enough, for paying guests to want to eat there. Just because you and your family like it doesn't mean your guests will. You have probably become blind to the clutter on the counter by the back door, on top of the refrigerator, on the refrigerator door, and on the window sill. Also, if you serve breakfast in your kitchen, you won't be able to use the kitchen for other chores (including cleaning up the breakfast pots and pans) while your guests are eating.

It's a good idea to have a door that separates the kitchen from the dining room. It makes the dining room seem more private for your guests and allows you some privacy in the kitchen to do the dishes, use the phone, talk with your children or spouse, or fold laundry.

Breakfast in Bed

There are B&Bs that serve breakfast in the guest rooms—"breakfast in bed"—as you yourself may have experienced. If you are considering offer-

ing this option, here are some reasons *not* to: Guests will spill things in the rooms, soiling or staining the beddings, rug, etc., which will make more work later for you and your helper. Crumbs left in the rooms are an invitation to ants and other pests. No matter how luxurious it may sound, eating breakfast in bed is awkward and less enjoyable than sitting at a table. Guests also benefit immensely from meeting the other guests at a B&B, whether they expect to or not, and you should not deprive them of the opportunity to broaden their horizons over breakfast. Breakfast is a good time for you to answer guests' questions about directions, restaurants, and shops, and give them whatever other information they need before they set off for the day. Finally, serving breakfast to each guest room will take more time than serving one or two seatings in your dining room, and the same is true for the cleaning up. If you really do want to make breakfast available in the guest rooms, provide a café table and chairs. For some couples, especially those on their honeymoon, this may seem wonderfully romantic.

How to Serve

Whether you are going to serve your guests yourself or let them serve themselves from a buffet, set the table to be as pretty and inviting as possible. Use your best china, linens, and silver. An arrangement of fresh flowers adds beauty and helps create an ambiance that is truly special. Put jams in pretty jam pots, milk and cream in pitchers, and baked goods in baskets. Set pastries on footed plates, and don't hesitate to decorate serving platters and dishes with fresh herbs and flowers from your garden. Fruit looks especially pretty in footed glass dishes, as do juices served in wine glasses. Classical music playing softly in the background adds to the festive feeling and helps fill any initial quiet moments when guests first meet one another. Place an attractive guest book and pen on the breakfast table for guests to sign on their last morning at your B&B. This is a distinctly different item from the register guests fill out at check-in time; here guests may write brief notes to you, comments and compliments, signing their names and home states. Many guests enjoy reading the other entries, seeing how far afield your guests hail from, and this elicits all kinds of good-spirited chatter. Last but not least, set the table properly (see illustration p. 99) and provide your guests with substantial, comfortable chairs at an uncrowded table.

If you are going to use a tablecloth, consider that real linen wears better and lasts longer, and immediately lends the air of a special occasion, making guests feel like VIPs. A table that is appealing aesthetically invites guests to be at their convivial best and enhances the food you serve. Whether you use tablecloths or place mats, you will need to have a few sets on hand in order to have fresh ones when needed. If you use cloth napkins, they should be cotton or linen. Polyester napkins, which do not absorb liquid, are really useless. Also, they don't launder as well as natural fibers and will hold stains more readily. A high-quality paper napkin is a fine alternative to linen and will cut down on the ironing you or your helper will have to do.

Serve your guests graciously, and train your helpers to do the same. The general rule of thumb is "serve from the left, take from the right," but it

is not ironclad. When pouring coffee or tea, stand on the right-hand side of your guest, lift the saucer, and hold it away from them as you pour, in case there is a spill. When pouring juice or water, hold the glass at the bottom; don't wrap your hand around the top of the glass. Be attentive to your guests, but let them enjoy their breakfast at their leisure; after all, they're on vacation. If you hover around the table, whisking away plates and glasses as soon as they are empty, your guests will feel hurried and uneasy.

One of the wonderful things about running a B&B is that you can dress more casually than you would at an office. Other than wearing something fresh and comfortable, I recommend that you invest in some professional chef's aprons (perhaps embroidered with your B&B name and logo) for you and your helpers. Anyone with long hair should keep it pulled back while preparing and serving food. And hands should be scrupulously clean and well groomed.

Should You Eat with Your Guests?

Some hosts join their guests for breakfast; the choice is completely up to you. There are reasons why you may want to do this, and as many why you may not. If you are an early riser, you may not want to wait two or three hours before breakfast. And if you are doing all the cooking and serving alone, it is virtually impossible to sit down with your guests for a full breakfast. By not joining your guests, you'll have a precious pocket of time while they are eating and chatting to catch up on some of your own chores. This is a good time to start the laundry, make phone calls, write confirmation letters, send out brochures, fill out a bank deposit slip, etc. You'll still have ample opportunity to visit with guests while you serve breakfast; this is usually a good time to give directions and to chat with guests about what they have planned for the day and how they liked the restaurant you recommended the night before. When you are certain that everyone is finished eating, clear the plates and sit down and join them for a cup of coffee. They'll be hoping you will!

Menus and Recipes

You should serve a slightly different menu each day. Some of your guests will be staying as long as a week; it is possible and desirable to serve them a different breakfast each day. Remember, whether you are serving a full or continental breakfast, this special meal is part of the reason your guests chose a B&B over a hotel or motel, so you won't want to let them down by offering them the same fare over and over. To produce a varied menu, there are certain staple items that you should have on hand at all times (see the chart on the facing page).

Prepare everything fresh that morning; after all, anyone can stop at a convenience store for a frozen muffin that has been heated in a microwave oven! And if you are just learning your way around the kitchen, here are some tips that will help make you a better cook:

- Follow the seasons when buying fruits and vegetables.
- Buy local fruits and vegetables whenever possible.
- Use real ingredients, like real maple syrup, not artificial imitations.
- Cook from scratch.

These habits will guarantee you good results and save you money at the same time.

If you're looking for menu and recipe ideas other than the handful offered here, pick up *The Bed & Breakfast Cookbook,* my first book about

The Well-Stocked Pantry

You'll need to have the following on hand, whether you serve a full or continental breakfast:

flour	yogurt
sugar	light cream or half-and-half
baking powder	
baking soda	coffee beans, regular and decaffeinated
vanilla extract	
raisins, currants, and other dried fruit	black tea and herbal tea
	sugar substitute
nuts	non-dairy creamer
spices—cinnamon, nutmeg, allspice, etc.	selection of cold cereals
	selection of hot cereals
butter	bread
eggs	fresh fruit in season
milk	jams, jellies, honey

For full breakfasts you will also need:

cheese	potatoes
herbs—fresh or dried	onions
bacon, sausage, ham	fresh vegetables in season

B&Bs. With more than three hundred recipes from B&Bs around the country, it's a great way to expand your repertoire, whether you serve a full or continental breakfast.

You should be ready to cater to guests with special dietary requests. You'll need to keep decaffeinated coffee on hand, as well as herb teas and sugar substitutes, and you should be able to put out a good breakfast for a vegetarian, including the nondairy vegan.

Here are a week's worth of menus for full breakfasts that would be appropriate for a B&B just about anywhere in the country. All the recipes can be found in *The Bed & Breakfast Cookbook;* one recipe for each day is included here. All menus should be served with choices of coffee or tea and a selection of jams and jellies; hot or cold cereal should be available too.

MONDAY

broiled grapefruit
corned beef hash with poached eggs
buttermilk biscuits
pineapple-lime blender drink

TUESDAY

strawberry-banana parfait
pecan pancakes with butter and maple syrup
sausage links
freshly squeezed orange juice

WEDNESDAY

three-melon salad topped with lime ice
baked eggs
broiled tomatoes
wheat toast
coffee strudel
grapefruit juice

THURSDAY

sautéed nectarines
orange waffles with butter and maple syrup
crisp bacon
banana frappe

FRIDAY

Blueberry Delight
cheese omelet
Parmesan potatoes
crisp bacon
wheat toast
Swedish coffee cake
prune juice

SATURDAY

fresh peach-raspberry yogurt parfait
stuffed French toast with strawberry syrup
sausage patties
orange Julius

SUNDAY

baked pears
quiche Lorraine
baked ham
scones
cranberry muffins
mimosas

Buttermilk Biscuits

This is a melt-in-your-mouth delicious biscuit recipe.

MAKES 12 BISCUITS

2 cups flour
1 teaspoon salt
½ teaspoon baking
    powder

¼ teaspoon baking soda
8 tablespoons shortening
¾ cup buttermilk

Preheat oven to 400 degrees.

In a large bowl sift together the flour, salt, baking powder, and baking soda. Cut in shortening until the mixture is coarsely blended; add buttermilk and stir only until dough leaves sides of bowl. Turn the dough onto floured board. Gently pat into ¾-inch thickness. Cut with biscuit cutter and place on an ungreased cookie sheet. Bake at 400 degrees for 10 to 12 minutes. Serve with butter, preserves, and honey.

Pecan Pancakes (Pancakes Supreme)

These unusual pancakes, not too sweet, have a nutty whole-grain flavor, and are wholesome and hearty.

SERVES 4

1 cup whole wheat flour
½ cup rolled oats
1 teaspoon baking
    powder
½ teaspoon cinnamon
¼ teaspoon nutmeg
1½ cups milk

1 egg
2 tablespoons oil
2 tablespoons honey
1 apple, peeled, cored, and
    grated
¼ cup pecans, chopped

In a large bowl mix together the flour, oats, baking powder, cinnamon, and nutmeg. In a separate bowl beat the milk, egg, oil, and honey; stir in the apple and pecans. Add the wet mixture to the dry ingredients. Mix well.

Cook the pancakes in a lightly oiled, hot skillet until golden on both sides. Serve hot, with butter and honey or syrup.

Baked Eggs with Herbs and Cheese

This is a delicious way to serve eggs and so rich that one per person is plenty.

SERVES 1

1 tablespoon melted butter
1 egg
1 tablespoon half-and-half
1 tablespoon grated sharp cheddar cheese

Pinch of Italian herbs, or fresh herbs of your choice
Parsley
Parmesan cheese, grated
Ground black pepper
Paprika

Preheat oven to 350 degrees.

Pour melted butter into an individual serving–sized ramekin or custard dish. Break the egg into the dish. Pour in the half-and-half. Sprinkle the grated cheddar cheese over the half-and-half. Sprinkle herbs, a pinch of parsley, a dusting of Parmesan cheese, a little ground black pepper, and paprika over top. Place ramekin in a baking dish; carefully add water until the ramekin is sitting in about ½ inch of water. Bake at 350 degrees for 20 minutes.

To serve, run a knife around the edge of the ramekin, drain off any excess liquid, and slip the baked egg onto a toasted English muffin half. Serve immediately.

Variation: The baked egg may be served on a muffin topped with Canadian bacon, a thick slice of tomato, or 2 pieces of crisp bacon.

Orange Waffles

These delicious waffles, with a subtle orange flavor, are crisp outside, fluffy inside. Wonderful for breakfast, but also suitable as a dessert waffle.

SERVES 6

2 cups flour
3 teaspoons baking
    powder
2 tablespoons sugar
½ teaspoon salt
4 eggs

1 cup milk
4 tablespoons butter,
    melted
3 tablespoons finely
    grated orange zest

In a large bowl sift together the flour, baking powder, sugar, and salt. In a separate bowl combine the eggs, milk, and butter; beat well. Add the orange zest to the egg mixture; pour this into the flour mixture, one half at a time, beating well after each addition until the batter is smooth.

Ladle into a hot, well-oiled waffle iron, and cook until waffles are golden. Keep waffles warm in the oven while making the rest. Serve hot, with butter, jams, and syrup.

Parmesan Potatoes

These tasty potatoes fill the kitchen with a wonderful aroma as they bake. At Palmer's Chart House, a B&B on Orcas Island, Washington, they are served for breakfast with Canadian bacon, eggs, and hot applesauce sprinkled with nutmeg.

SERVES 8

6 medium potatoes	1 teaspoon salt
½ cup grated Parmesan	1 teaspoon pepper
cheese	4 tablespoons butter
¼ cup flour	

Preheat oven to 350 degrees.

Peel the potatoes and cut each into eight pieces. Combine the Parmesan cheese, flour, salt, and pepper into a paper bag. Place the potatoes in the bag, hold the top shut, and shake. Put the butter into a 9-x-13-inch pan; place in the preheated oven until butter melts, remove and add the coated potatoes. Toss lightly. Bake at 350 degrees for 30 minutes. Use a spatula to turn the potatoes over, then bake for an additional 30 minutes. Serve hot.

Orange Julius

"This beverage is juice, milk, dessert, and table decoration all in one when served in an oversized red-wine glass and garnished with an orange slice and sprig of mint," says Louise Sims of The Bells B&B in Bethlehem, New Hampshire.

SERVES 6

· 6 ounces frozen orange juice concentrate	½ cup sugar
1 cup milk	1 teaspoon vanilla
1 cup water	12 ice cubes, crushed

Place all ingredients in a blender and process at high speed for 30 seconds. Serve immediately.

Variation: Substitute frozen pineapple juice for the orange juice.

Baked Pears Hersey

Baked Pears Hersey—from Hersey House B&B in Ashland, Oregon— takes advantage of the local fruit and is very popular with guests. This dish may be served at breakfast or as an elegant light dessert after a rich dinner.

SERVES 8

4 pears, halved, cored, and peeled	4 tablespoons brown sugar
¼ teaspoon cinnamon	Topping (optional):
⅛ teaspoon nutmeg	whipped cream or
4 tablespoons butter, softened	vanilla yogurt

Preheat oven to 350 degrees.

Place the pear halves in a greased pie plate, cut side down and arranged like spokes with the narrow ends pointed toward the center. Sprinkle the pears with the cinnamon and nutmeg. Cover and set aside.

In a small bowl combine the butter and brown sugar thoroughly, and then carefully spread the mixture over the pears.

Bake at 350 degrees for 20 to 25 minutes. Serve warm. Top with whipped cream or vanilla yogurt, if you like.

You will have your own favorite family recipes that you'll want to serve at breakfast. When you visit other B&Bs, take some breakfast menu and recipe ideas home with you. It's important to keep expanding the variety of your breakfast choices to keep your menu interesting for you and your guests.

As a busy host, you'll make your job easier if you are organized. If at all possible, set the table for the next day as soon as your guests finish breakfast and the table is cleared. Keep a well-stocked pantry, freezer, and refrigerator. Have made-from-scratch master mixes on hand for biscuits, muffins, and pancakes, and keep a few loaves of quick bread in your freezer. You should do most of your baking fresh each morning, but certain dense quick breads—pumpkin, cranberry, banana, and others—are none the worse for being frozen and come in handy on those mornings when a small crisis erupts.

Make breakfast a special occasion in every way for your guests, and they will start their day marveling over their good fortune in finding you and your enticing B&B.

7

House Rules and Safety Features

---

*B*e prepared.
— MOTTO OF THE BOY SCOUTS
OF AMERICA

Rules, Rules, Rules

*T*he purpose of house rules at your bed-and-breakfast is to make the time that your guests are with you more pleasant and safe for them and for you. Experienced B&B travelers expect to find some limitations on what they can and cannot do, and by making these rules clear and simple, you ensure that you and your guests can relax and enjoy yourselves more easily and completely.

You should establish your house rules *before* you open for business, although after you've been running your B&B for a while, you may decide to change or add to them. A good way to get some ideas on what your house rules should cover at a minimum is to visit other B&Bs and see what are common restrictions. Make mental notes, or jot the rules down, and when you are home, ask yourself which ones you want to adopt for your business.

Smoking

Probably the most common house rule at B&Bs is a restriction on smoking. If you are a smoker, then you really should allow guests to smoke in some part of your house. But whether you are a smoker or not, you should not allow smoking in the guest rooms. The odor will become a permanent fixture in the room—distasteful to many travelers—and a startling number of house fires are caused by careless smoking. For these two reasons alone, this is an essential house rule, and one that B&B travelers have come to expect. Now you must decide if you are going to allow smoking *anywhere* inside. Plenty of B&Bs say "smoking outside only." If you are going to allow smoking inside, you should have more than one common room for guests and allow smoking in only one of them. That way, guests who find cigarette smoke offensive won't be forced to retreat to their rooms when a smoker settles in to watch the evening news in your one common room. It is perfectly acceptable to allow smoking outdoors only; if you do, there should be some kind of outdoor "room" with a table and chairs so that your guests who smoke aren't forced to stand at the curb with their cigarette, feeling like a bad dog who's been banished from the house. Porches and patios are a good place to allow smoking; be sure to have an ashtray or two on the tables, and empty and clean them daily.

Off-Limits

Often house rules will mention which rooms the guests may use. These are the common rooms or public rooms referred to in chapter 5, and it is quite easy to tell guests, without being rude about it, that their wanderings in the house are restricted. For instance, you may say something like, "Please make yourself at home in the living room that adjoins the dining room, or in the second-floor sitting room, which has a television." This implies that even if guests have glimpsed your family room off the kitchen, it is clearly off-limits to them. For travelers who are new to bed-and-breakfasts, it is reassuring to be told that they *are* welcome to use the living room. These restrictions may apply to the yard as well. If there is a portion of the yard that is for you and your family only, and another area you want guests to use, you'll need to say so in the house rules. If you decide to give your guests free range over your entire property, point that out too, so that guests can get the most out of their stay and not accidentally discover on their last day that they could have been enjoying your acres of wildflowers. Decide which parts of your property (inside and out) you want guests to know they can or cannot use, and state your decision in a clear, friendly manner in the house rules.

Curfew

Although you won't have a curfew, it's a good idea to state politely in your house rules that, as a courtesy to others in the house, guests coming and going after 10:00 P.M. (or whatever hour you choose) should be as quiet as possible. A brief mention of this is all that's needed to remind most travelers that they are not staying in a motel.

Phone Privileges

If there is a phone for guests and you do not have one in each guest room, it's a good idea to include this information in the house rules too. That way, guests who are uncertain of your policy won't have to track you down before making a call.

Kitchen Access

Couples who are staying at your B&B to celebrate an anniversary may want to chill some champagne. If you have a small refrigerator just for guests, as some B&Bs do, be sure to mention it in the rules. If you don't, but are willing to let guests have limited use of your refrigerator for chilling wine, etc., you may want to tell them so when guests check in and you are showing them the house.

Check-out

You will have to establish a check-out time for guests; post it in your house rules as a reminder. Although there will be guests who ignore check-out time, having it in black and white will be very helpful for you should you need to gently reinforce your rule.

Parking

You will need to provide off-street parking for your guests, and unless your parking area is very obvious from outside, you will need to put a note about it in your house rules. You don't want guests inadvertently blocking a neighbor's driveway or getting a ticket for parking illegally on the street overnight.

Keys

The door that your guests will use coming and going from your B&B should be kept locked, so guests will need keys. Since some people are not in the habit of locking their houses and will leave without their key, you could save yourself some trouble by reminding guests that they need their house key *whenever* they go out, whether they think you are home or not.

Miscellaneous

You need to consider how you feel about your guests bringing friends (nonguests) back to the B&B to socialize. You probably won't mind if your guests return with the relatives they have come to your town to visit, but other scenarios—not all pleasant—need to be anticipated. For instance, how would you feel if a guest came back with a newfound friend to "entertain" him or her at your B&B? Here's an example: A single gentleman returning around midnight made so much noise trying to get in the front door (he was intoxicated) that I went down to see if he had lost his house key. He had another man with him whom he'd met at a bar and invited to use the "empty" room available at my B&B. There *had* been one empty room when my guest left for the evening, but in the meantime it had been taken and was occupied! Needless to say, I told the uninvited guest that I no longer had a vacant room, and he stumbled off down the road. On another occasion I had a couple who were spending a weekend at my B&B return from a day at the beach with another couple they knew from their hometown (a two-hour drive). They had invited these people, whom they

hadn't expected to see, back to the B&B to shower and change before the long drive home. I happened to be in the house when my guests returned and asked me for more bath towels for their friends! This was a very awkward situation for me; I wanted to say no but did not want to appear rude. This extra couple would be using hot water, and I didn't want my other guests who were still out to end up with cold showers. I also didn't like the idea of strangers whom I knew nothing about roaming around my house. Now my house rules include a note that says, "In consideration of other guests, we ask that you check with us before bringing anyone back to the B&B for socializing."

Making Your Own Rules

These are the house rules that you will probably want to include, along with a few others that you need, to make *your* B&B work best for you. Each bed-and-breakfast is unique, so don't be afraid to include a rule that you've never seen at another B&B if it seems important to you. Brainstorm with family members about these restrictions; they may think of an issue you've overlooked.

Keep It Simple

Decide on your house rules carefully, then word them clearly and politely and have them printed. It's important that the rules can be quickly and easily read and understood and that the tone is friendly and gracious. If you have trouble phrasing the rules you've decided on, enlist the help of the same person who is going to help you design your brochure. Your house rules should fit on one page, and you'll need one for each guest room. These can then be put in an attractive picture frame and placed on the dresser or somewhere else in the room where they are easily seen. Another option is to put the framed rules on the inside of the bedroom door. Do not place a typed sheet of rules on the bedside table; it will soon become dog-eared or disappear altogether.

Many of the items included in your list of house rules are things that you will normally mention casually to guests when they check in and you are showing them around. But you *still* need to have the rules in writing;

there will be times when guests check in very late at night and it's all you can do to show them to their room, much less run through the house rules, or if you have helpers checking guests in, you can't count on them always to remember to mention all the house rules. Don't assume that guests will automatically know when they are intruding in a part of the house you don't want them to use or doing something else you had hoped they wouldn't. If the rules are in black and white, clearly visible in each guest room, you can rest assured that your guests will know what's expected of them whether you remember to tell them or not.

In the Event of Fire

While not a rule, instructions in the event of fire are essential information that should always be included at the end of your list of house rules. There should be a way to exit directly from each guest room; this exit should be clearly described under the caption "In the Event of Fire" at the bottom of the page.

Rules of Operation

In addition to house rules, which you devise to make your B&B operation run smoothly when your guests are there, you'll need to consider what other restrictions you want to impose *before* guests arrive.

Children

For instance, will you accept children, and if so, of what age? Collecting brochures from other B&Bs to get ideas on these restrictions (as well as design ideas for your own brochure), you'll find that B&Bs that don't accept young children are the norm, not the exception. You may decide to accept children twelve years and older, ten and older, or children of any age, including infants: it's completely up to you. But if you decide to accept children under eight years of age, keep in mind that they may bother other guests who are on a much-needed and barely afforded vacation from their own youngsters. Many B&B hosts say, "Kids are fine; it's the parents who are the problem." All parents will tell you that their chil-

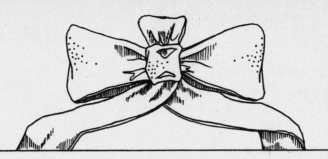

House Rules

While you are here, please observe these house rules:

Smoking is not allowed in the house. You may smoke on the patio in the back of the house.

In addition to your own quarters, please make yourself at home in the living room, sun room, or patio while you are here.

There is a buffet-style continental breakfast available in the dining room from 8:00 A.M. to 9:30 A.M. Early risers may help themselves to coffee or tea from 7:00 A.M. on.

If you come in late at night, please be as quiet as possible. Others may be sleeping.

There is a telephone in the foyer for your use.

The house is always locked. Remember to take your key whenever you go out.

There is off-street parking in back of the house; please do not park on the street.

In consideration of other guests, please check with us before bringing anyone back to the B&B for socializing.

On your last morning, checkout time is 11:00 A.M.

In the Event of Fire:

If you are unable to exit the house via the stairs, return to your room, close the door, and use the chain ladder provided in your closet and exit via your window. There is a flashlight in the top drawer of your bedside table.

dren are well behaved, but that doesn't mean you'll agree. And babies cry in the night (they can't help it!), make dirty diapers that are left in the bathroom (if it's shared, this is a *problem*), and throw food around the dining room. Kids will generally be noisier than adults and, if they're toddlers, may increase your liability.

If these facts haven't discouraged you from accepting kids, you must now consider what you will charge for them. Your rates will be based on double occupancy or single occupancy. Parents with young children often want them to share the room (you'll need rollaways or cots) and want them to stay free. Since you'll still be providing sheets, towels, breakfast, etc., free is not a good idea. What will you charge per child? Find out what other B&Bs in your area that accept children charge per child. If you're going to limit your B&B to children twelve and older, you may also want to say that children do not share a room but have their own room and pay the full rate, or you can discount the two rooms at a "family rate" (more about that in the next chapter).

Pets

There are B&Bs that accept pets; perhaps you've stayed at one. I advise against accepting pets because you'll be opening yourself up to all kinds of liability (what if a guest's dog bites another guest?); dogs and cats have fleas; some people are allergic to animals; and animals in the guest rooms will make more work for you to clean up later. You may not have thought that this restriction was even one you'd need to consider, but you will be surprised at the number of callers who want to know if they can bring their pet. Perhaps you can recommend a kennel in the area. In any case, have an answer ready for them.

Forms of Payment

You will need to decide whether you'll accept credit cards for payment, or personal checks, or cash or traveler's checks only. Credit cards require paperwork and are an added expense. If, however, you are going to have a large operation, you will probably want to offer this amenity. You'll find from reading brochures, and from your own travels, that some B&Bs

accept personal checks only for deposits; final payment must be made with cash. The decision is yours, but you'll need to make it before you open for business.

Deposits

How large a deposit you'll require is another matter to decide before opening for business. Follow the lead of most B&Bs: a 50 percent deposit, or minimum one-night deposit—received within one week of the date the reservation is made—is required to confirm and hold a reservation. In other words, if a caller reserves a room for four nights at the rate of $75 per night, you will ask him to send you a 50 percent deposit—in this case, $150. But if the caller is reserving a room for only one night at the rate of $75, you will want a deposit in the full amount, because a one-night deposit is the *minimum* required to hold a reservation. You will find this is standard policy at nearly every B&B (as well as hotels and resorts).

Cancellation/Refund Policy

You will also need to work out a cancellation and refund policy. Once a deposit is received and the reservation is confirmed, most B&Bs require that at least fourteen days' notice be given to cancel a reservation in order for a full refund (minus a small processing fee, usually fifteen dollars) to be given. Cancellations received fewer than fourteen days prior to arrival are subject to more restrictions, most often that the deposit will be refunded only if the room can be rebooked. Even if the room is rebooked, the processing fee is deducted from any refund.

Check-in

As mentioned earlier, you will post check-out time in the house rules, but you will also need to decide on a check-in time. Eleven A.M. is a standard check-out time; check-in varies more, but if your check-out time is 11:00 A.M., checking in should not start any sooner than 1:00 P.M. or 2:00 P.M. You'll need those hours to clean the rooms and take care of other chores before new guests arrive. Most B&Bs put a limit on check-in times; quite often brochures will read, "Check-in between 2:00 and 10:00 P.M." Of course, guests who are forced to arrive later will still be allowed to check in, but by establishing some kind of limit, you are laying a ground rule that most travelers will be able to follow, and in the process you will be helping create a schedule for yourself or your helper.

These are the kinds of things that you'll put in your brochure. Undoubtedly, you will refine your rules and procedures after you've been in business for a while, but starting with these basics helps ensure that you'll begin operation with as few untoward situations as possible.

A Safe House

Many of the issues that you will address to keep your B&B running smoothly are also issues of safety, for both you and your guests. Ask yourself how to make your house a safe place for guests, thereby limiting the likelihood of accidents and mishaps, and limiting your liability at the same time. Accidents *do* happen, but if you've readied your house carefully, you are less likely to be found negligent.

Fire Safety

Start by asking the fire chief to inspect your home, even if you are buying an established B&B. Ask him to bring along copies of the state and local fire codes so that you'll have them to refer to later. Begin in the basement and walk through the house with him, room by room, taking notes as you go, writing down each recommendation he makes. Point out to him which rooms are guest bedrooms, and let him know what your maximum occupancy will be. Ask lots of questions (it's a good idea to make out a list before he gets there) and don't hesitate to ask for explanations and details on matters that you don't understand. Unless the fire chief customarily issues certificates of good standing after inspecting a house, ask him to send you a written verification of the inspection he has performed at your B&B. If he won't write the verification until you've made certain changes and improvements, make those and have him back for a follow-up inspection. Then file copies of the inspection report with your insurance agent and in your business files. Thereafter, have the inspection repeated every year so that your certificate is up-to-date.

The first recommendation that the fire chief is likely to make is that there be smoke detectors in the house. He'll advise you which rooms need them and where to place them. There are lots of different ones available; ask which style or brand he recommends and why. There are both battery-operated smoke detectors and units that are wired into your electrical circuits. There are even smoke detectors that can be wired to sound an alarm at the local fire department (these are more expensive but have their advantages). Compare all the options, and with the suggestions from your fire chief and insurance agent, choose what is best for your operation.

If you are going to have a large bed-and-breakfast—say, six guest rooms or more—the fire chief may recommend a sprinkler system. This option is, obviously, more expensive than installing smoke detectors, but if you are in the process of extensive renovations or building new, it might be a worthwhile choice. Generally, having a sprinkler system will lower your insurance rates; that savings may help offset the initial cost enough to sway your decision. If you are building or renovating a house for B&B purposes, it's a good idea to get the fire chief's ideas and criticisms before you go forward with plans. Although architects and builders should be aware of fire codes and general safety features, don't make decisions based on their word alone; talk to the person whose business it is to know these things—your fire chief.

Other areas that your fire chief will want to discuss with you are the wiring, lighting, and emergency exits in your house. The recommendations may all start to sound overly cautious, but you'll be glad you've followed them if there is ever an emergency.

If it's possible to have your insurance agent present during the fire chief's inspection, do so. It will save you from covering a lot of the same ground twice and may help you get better advice than if each were to tour your B&B separately.

Make sure that all stairs, inside and out, are safe. They should be well lit and in sound condition. Old, tattered, or loose carpet could cause a guest to trip and fall, as could a rotted board on a porch step. Outside steps should not be slippery; if they are painted, use a nonskid sand mixture made for this purpose. All stairways should have rugged handrails, and if they are wide enough, one on each side.

Locks

At the very least, guest bedroom doors should lock from the inside, so that when guests are in their rooms they are protected from intruders. If your guests are also able to lock their doors behind them when they go out, there is less likelihood that any of their things could be stolen. In most instances the door that guests use coming and going from your B&B (and *all* entrance/exit doors to the house, for that matter, depending on your location and setting) should be kept closed and locked. Give your guests keys when they check in and explain that they will need to take their house key whenever they go out. This precaution is for your guests' safety, and it also limits your liability. Realize that if you run a fairly small operation without someone on duty at all times, strangers who spot your B&B sign and are looking for lodging will walk right in your house without knocking if the front door is not locked. This can be a bit disconcerting if you don't hear them enter and first meet them as you are dashing from your shower to your bedroom!

Bathroom Safety

Bathrooms are another potential problem area. The shower or tub should have a rubber mat in it to help prevent slipping, and there should be grab bars as well (these are often built into new showers and are standard equipment on shower doors). The electrical outlet must be GFI, which stands for "ground fault interrupter," and which is designed to trip its circuit automatically to prevent accidental electrocution if the appliance in use comes in contact with water.

Drugs, Alcohol, and Allergic Reactions

I once attended a B&B seminar where one of the speakers, a liability expert, advised us never to give *any* over-the-counter drugs to guests who asked for them—even aspirin! He told us that a guest who had an allergic reaction to the drug we supplied would have grounds for a lawsuit. (It might not hold up in court, but in today's litigious world, who knows!) So I always pass along the advice. Chances are there is a pharmacy or supermarket nearby; you can say that you are out of the item in question—aspirin, cough syrup, and the like—and direct your guest to the closest place to purchase it.

Travelers with food allergies should certainly make them known to their host, but in case they don't, this is another good reason to ask your guests about any particular likes or dislikes they may have when you tell them about breakfast. That's their cue to tell you they are allergic to yeast, or corn products, or whatever.

Along the same lines, professionals in liability management will advise hosts not to serve guests alcohol. Chances are you have stayed at B&Bs where the hosts offered you a glass of sherry or wine in the evening (some B&Bs even mention this in their advertising and brochures). So what should *you* do? Use your best judgment. What you are trying to avoid, obviously, is being held responsible for getting a guest intoxicated who subsequently goes out and gets in a car accident or being the cause of a guest tripping and falling in your house after one too many. Although you shouldn't make it a regular habit to offer alcohol to every guest, you may

decide to bend the rules in certain circumstances. Even then, never give a guest more than *one* drink.

A Dog in the House

If you have a dog, you should not give it the run of the house, for a number of reasons. For one thing, dogs shed, and you'll be doing enough vacuuming as it is, trying to keep your house up to B&B standards of cleanliness. For another, many people are slightly allergic to dogs; these people will stay at a B&B with a dog that is confined to a back yard and family room—areas that guests don't use—but not a B&B where the dog may be right outside their door. And as even the most devoted animal lover should know and admit, on occasion even the best dogs have been known to bite strangers. You can't take this chance with your B&B.

A Matter of Life and Death

Your local hospital probably offers CPR courses on a regular basis. If you haven't done so already, sign up and take one. You may never need it, but it's a good skill to have.

Insurance

Have your insurance agent come to your house to discuss the coverage you are going to need once you are running a B&B. Ask for specific guidelines on reducing your liability from an insurance point of view, and get everything in writing. You will need more than your old homeowner's policy, even with an extra liability umbrella. There are a number of companies offering insurance designed specifically for bed-and-breakfasts (see the appendix for resources). If your agent is unfamiliar with these programs, you'll have to do more research on your own. Make some comparisons between policies and be sure you understand exactly what kind of coverage is offered. Do *not* start your business until you have the proper insurance in place.

What you are trying to do as you examine these safety issues is to make your house as safe and comfortable as possible for your guests and to avoid being found negligent if there ever is a mishap that leads to a lawsuit. If you carefully and thoroughly ensure safe conditions, you'll be able to enjoy your business more, knowing that your guests' well-being is as protected as it can be.

Protecting Your Own Valuables

The last safety issue to address is one you may not have thought of: how will *you* and your *own* valuables be protected once you let the world come walking through your front door? I'm glad to say that B&B travelers are a very nice bunch, and I've yet to meet a host who's had more than a bath towel stolen. There are a number of things you can and should do, however, now that your home will also be a temporary home to travelers. Your insurance policy should completely cover all your valuables; if needed, you should have extra riders for things like silver flatware, jewelry, art, and antiques. Any item that is so special or of such great sentimental value that it is, in your eyes, irreplaceable, should not be displayed in a room accessible to guests.

You may want to consider having a security system installed. Since your guests will have keys if you don't have someone on duty at the front desk at all times, the system wouldn't interfere with your guests' comings and goings. Sometimes a discreet decal on the front door, stating that the house is protected by a security system, is the best deterrent.

Your bedroom door should lock from the outside, just like the doors in your guest rooms, and you should lock that door and those to any other rooms that are for family use only whenever you go out. This small investment will give you great peace of mind.

If you set the breakfast table with sterling silver flatware and worry that it might be stolen, keep it in a locked drawer in your dining room sideboard. You can likewise lock away other valuables that you want to use on a daily basis, and even though they will be completely insured against loss of any kind, you will feel more at ease knowing you've made things a bit more difficult for any would-be thief.

As stated, I've yet to meet a host who has suffered any great loss to guests; travelers who frequent B&Bs are, by and large, a wonderful group. But if you've carefully planned against any possible misfortune, you and your family are much more likely to enjoy this delightful profession to the fullest.

8

Rates, Advertising, Reservations

What we obtain too cheap, we
esteem too lightly; it is dearness
only that gives everything its value.
—THOMAS PAINE

How to Figure Your Rates

*E*stablishing room rates will be one of the most important decisions you'll make before opening for business, and it is one that stumps many new hosts. It's really not that difficult, as you'll see; there are some easy steps to follow in determining what your rates should be.

First off, find out what the other B&Bs in your town and surrounding area are charging and what they are offering at those rates. The best way to do that is to collect brochures and rate sheets; if you call and ask for rate information and identify yourself as the soon-to-be new host in town, some hosts will be less than honest with you, especially those who view you as competition. You may have to enlist out-of-town friends or relatives to do some of this work for you. Describing themselves as potential guests, they can call or write the local B&Bs, requesting their brochures and rates, and then pass that information along to you. Once you've gathered the information, you've got something realistic to compare your own establishment to, and this comparison will help immensely in deciding what your rates should be, at least initially.

Find out what the motels and hotels in your area are charging for double- and single-occupancy rooms. Look at the rooms in person, using the pretense that you have family coming to town and you're investigating lodging for them. When you leave, take the brochure and rate sheet with you.

Be careful when you look at the rates other B&Bs are charging; just because a B&B in your town is charging one hundred dollars a night for a double-occupancy room doesn't mean that you can too. If their rooms have private baths and fireplaces, and they serve a full breakfast, versus your rooms with no fireplaces and a continental breakfast, your rates *should* be lower than theirs. The reverse is true as well; don't let an area B&B with low rates discourage you from setting yours higher if your B&B has more amenities, larger rooms, and a better location.

Amenities and Rates

Next, ask yourself what *you'll* be offering *your* B&B guests. Do your rooms have private baths or shared, or do you have some of each? Rooms with a private bath are worth more than rooms with a shared bath. Will you be serving a full breakfast or continental? A full breakfast allows you to charge higher rates than a continental. Will you be offering afternoon tea? If so, your rates can be higher. Do you have extensive public rooms or grounds for your guests to use? If the answer is yes, your rates should be higher than that of a B&B down the street that has one small living room for family and guests. Are your guest bedrooms small, with enough room for a bed but not much more, or are they roomy enough to include a sitting area? Obviously, larger rooms are worth more than small ones, and travelers are willing to pay more for them. Do your bedrooms have televisions, fireplaces, spectacular views, private balconies or patios, Jacuzzi tubs, or other special amenities? Any one of these allows you to charge more for the room, and if you offer all of them, your room rates can be downright pricey.

The Market

Another consideration is what the market will bear in your area. Your rooms and amenities may be every bit as nice as those offered by that spectacular B&B you stayed at in California's Sonoma Valley wine region. But your little town in eastern Connecticut just can't command that kind of price. It's a mistake to compare rates from B&Bs you've visited to the rates you're planning on charging if the areas are vastly different in market prices. The cost of real estate, restaurants, and other goods and services will give you all the clues you need.

Fine-Tuning

Once you have a general idea of what your rates should be, you'll need to fine-tune them. If your B&B is in a resort area, you'll find that other lodging establishments have different rates for different times of the year. Even if you're not going to be open year-round, you'll probably want to establish a range of rates—low-season, high-season, weekday, and weekend. Again, see what the range is at the other B&Bs, inns, and hotels in your area. If you find that low-season rates are generally ten to twenty dollars less per night than high-season, with a similar difference between weekday and weekend, then your rates should probably reflect something pretty close to that standard. Don't lower your rates too much, though, or you may find yourself operating in the red. If the winter months will be your low season, for instance, the expense of heating guest rooms will take a bite out of your profits. Your operating costs may actually be higher during your low season, but travelers will expect reduced rates. As long as your off-season rates are reasonable, and you're still making enough profit to make it worth your while, you can take comfort in the fact that you are building a clientele: many of these off-season visitors will be back again during peak season, and they will tell their friends about you too.

Many B&Bs (as well as inns, hotels, and motels) have minimum stay requirements during certain times of the week or year. It is not unusual, for instance, to find a three-night minimum for such holiday weekends as New Year's, Fourth of July, and Labor Day. Find out what's done in your area and don't be afraid to instate those rules at your business, even though at first you may be tempted to accept any reservation you can get. Also, consider an extra charge for the holidays; a ten-dollar-per-night surcharge is not unusual, as you will find doing your research. In addition to minimum stay requirements on holidays, many B&Bs have a two-night minimum on peak-season weekends. To give yourself and your guests a little more flexibility, you may want to follow the lead of B&Bs who advertise that "subject to availability, a stay of only one night may be arranged with a 50 percent surcharge."

Discounts

If your B&B is likely to attract more guests on weekends than during the week, it's a good idea to offer lower rates for midweek stays; this policy helps fill your rooms, and many of these guests will return again on a weekend. The reverse of this is true for B&Bs located in cities. You will find that business travelers (probably the bulk of your clientele) need rooms during the week, while the weekends are quiet. By offering lower rates on the weekends, you can keep your rooms filled all week long.

If you are not going to have a B&B that caters mostly to business travelers, you may want to consider offering a discount for midweek stays of three or more nights. This is just one more way to help fill rooms, and since there is much less work for you on days when there is no change of guests, you can justify the discount.

Families usually look for some kind of discount, especially if they will be reserving two or more rooms and want them for a stay of more than two nights. If you are not going to accept young children at your B&B, then you probably don't need to figure out a family rate. But if you will be taking children of some ages and you have guest room arrangements where two bedrooms connect to a shared bath (perfect for a family), you should plan what kind of a discounted rate you will offer to a family. The discount will

be good for your business, and quite often the parents will come back for another visit without the kids and will then be paying your normal rate.

Parents traveling with one young child will want the child to stay in their room. This means you will need a rollaway or cot for the child, and you need to figure out what to charge for it. As of this writing, anywhere from fifteen to thirty dollars added on to the standard double-occupancy room rate is the norm for a child sharing a room with parents. The lower rates are for B&Bs that offer only continental breakfast and have fewer other amenities as well. If you will be accepting children, figure out your rates in advance. You will be amazed at how many callers expect children to stay free. I don't know of any B&Bs that accept children free of charge, and I don't recommend that you do either. After all, you are providing not just the cot, but the bedding, extra bath towels, and an extra breakfast of some sort.

Senior citizens sometimes ask for a senior citizen discount. I have found a handful of B&Bs that include one in their rate sheet. Decide in advance whether you want to offer one; otherwise you may be momentarily flustered when a caller asks for it.

If you plan on not offering any discounts for seniors or families, be prepared to explain why to callers. You can say something like, "I've set my rates as low as I can with all that I provide my guests. I think you'll find when you call around that these rates are very reasonable. My rooms are twenty-five dollars less per night than the hotel in town [or whatever the case may be], and the hotel rate doesn't include breakfast." Some callers are very pushy about demanding discounts, and you'll want to be ready to handle them in a calm, friendly way.

Credit Cards

Decide before opening for business if you will accept credit cards. If so, you may want to raise your rates slightly. You'll have more paperwork each month, but travelers are willing to pay a little more to stay at a B&B that allows them the convenience of using a credit card. Some B&Bs state in their rate sheets that credit cards entail a small extra charge (usually 5 percent or a flat fee). You can find out what's involved by calling the major credit card companies; if you have a large-enough establishment, it will probably be worth your while to offer this extra.

Staying Competitive

Now that you know how to figure out your rates, my advice is to keep them a bit on the low side for your first season in business, unless you are purchasing an existing B&B. You will get more bookings this way and can look forward to raising your rates the next season, when the world knows you're there. It's also unlikely that you'll have all the kinks worked out that first season (whether you realize it now or not), and guests are willing to overlook a few small things if the rates are low. When rates are at the top of the spectrum, travelers expect something extraordinary; they will be unforgiving if everything is not perfect.

Taxes

You will probably need to add on a state tax and in some states an additional "room" tax to your rates. That information should be included on your rate sheet. As you'll find when you research other brochures, the tax rate is usually stated simply at the bottom of the page: "All rates are subject to a (whatever percent) tax."

Advertising

As you get ready to open your B&B, you need to do some advertising to let the public know you are there. Advertising can be expensive, however, so you need to determine how much you should do.

For your first year (unless you are buying an existing B&B), spend your advertising dollars conservatively. After all, you may find after one season that this business is not for you, and in that case, it would be a waste to have paid to be in half a dozen guidebooks, for instance. Find out from a couple of established B&B hosts in your area which advertising they have found to be most worthwhile, and use that as a starting point. You will probably want to increase your advertising over the next two or three years, as you learn where the dollars can be most effectively spent.

Tourism Departments

One of the first places to start should be with your local chamber of commerce. Although you may never have thought of this, your chamber of commerce (especially if you live in a resort area) is an excellent source of advertising. The annual fee to belong, and therefore to be listed as lodging, is usually very small and is an expenditure that can pay for itself many times over. Additionally, your town may have a tourism office, another good outlet for you to take advantage of, as advertising there is usually free or very inexpensive.

Your state will have a tourism department that publishes all kinds of pamphlets and brochures to try to lure travelers (and their money) to your state. Be sure to list your B&B with them; there is usually no charge.

Guidebooks

Visit your library and favorite bookstore and look at the bed-and-breakfast guidebooks available. There is a wide variety; some are regional and others cover the entire United States. At the bookstore ask which guidebooks have been the best sellers. Then pick one regional and one national edition that most appeal to you. The information you'll need to write to the author or publisher—so that your B&B can be included in the next edition—will be inside the book, either at the front or the back. There is usually a fee for the listing (something that surprises most people), but if you find that a particular guide brings you a lot of bookings, the fee is well worth it. These books are usually updated every other year, and you will pay a fee each time, if one is charged. See the appendix, page 183, for a listing of some of the best-selling B&B guidebooks.

Obviously, it will be a year before your B&B will appear in any of these guidebooks, at the soonest. So you still need to find other forms of advertising that can yield immediate results.

Magazines

Certain magazines publish special travel guide editions every year, either in the spring or fall. If you live in New England, for instance, *Yankee* magazine publishes a New England travel guide each spring that sells millions of copies. This is an excellent place to advertise; everyone who buys it is planning on traveling in New England that season, and one of the things they are looking for is lodging. It is a handsome publication, and the name Yankee Publishing lends it a lot of credibility. Although it is a fairly expensive place to advertise, your money will probably be well spent. You can make it more affordable by placing an ad with a group of other area bed-and-breakfasts. Visit a bookstore or newsstand in your town to see which magazine publisher puts out such a guide for your part of the country. Then call one of the advertising representatives for information and rates. You should be able to get into the upcoming edition, unless it is about to be published. In any event, it will be faster than getting into a B&B guidebook.

Certain magazines are written expressly for travelers, and if you have a large-enough operation, you may decide the cost is worth it for you to advertise in one of them a few times a year. *Country Inns/Bed & Breakfast* is a beautifully produced magazine with a good circulation, and it targets an audience of avid B&B fans. Again, to help reduce your cost, consider getting a group of local B&Bs to go in on the ad with you. The magazine's ad representative will be able to help you compose and design an attractive advertisement.

You may want to target magazines other than general travel publications. If you live in a great winter skiing area, for instance, you should review some of the ski magazines on the market. It may be worth it to forgo the general travel group and zero in on your specific audience.

Newspapers

Newspapers can be another good place to advertise, but you'll want to be selective. You'll probably want to advertise not in your local paper, but rather in the largest major newspaper for your area. For instance, even if you live in New Hampshire, it could be worthwhile for you to advertise with the *Boston Globe.* Contact the major newspaper for the closest large metropolitan area and talk to someone in the advertising department about listings in their Sunday travel supplements. It may sound pointless to advertise so close to home, but it isn't. Quick, short getaways are becoming the most popular vacations with Americans, particularly the baby boomers, and most newspapers have recognized this. A few times a year, established B&Bs within the circulation area are solicited to advertise in special travel sections that are going to be published at appropriate times. The fee is relatively small, and you'll want to try a listing like this at least once or twice.

The Phone Book

The yellow pages of your telephone directory are another place to advertise, simply by having your phone number listed there. You *will* get business, indirectly, from people who live in your area; they will have friends and family coming to town whom they have no room to house. They may not have noticed your B&B, especially if it is in an out-of-the-way location, but they'll know you're there when they spot your number in the yellow pages under "Bed-and-Breakfast."

Nearly Free Advertising

Because you will be getting business in this way from local people, a good and virtually free form of advertising is to post your brochure and business card on the bulletin boards of local churches, civic organizations, exercise clubs, schools, and the like. Make sure the local bridal shops have your brochures on hand. You'll be pleasantly surprised how much business all of this advertising will bring you.

If there are any boarding schools, colleges, or universities in your area, be sure to contact the alumni and admissions offices. Keep them supplied with your brochures and business cards; they can send a lot of business your way. Get copies of their events calendars so that you know when homecoming weekend, freshman orientation, graduation, and the like are,

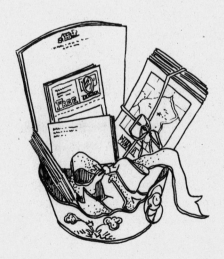

and mark those on your reservation calendar. Those are times when you'll want to require two-night minimum bookings, and possibly at a higher than normal rate.

An attractive and visible B&B sign is a good and inexpensive way to advertise. If you live on a well-traveled street, a sign will bring people who like to travel without reservations right to your door. During your first year in business, such guests can be a great boon and can account for 25 to 30 percent of your bookings. Even if you don't have a room for them, they will leave with your brochure and may call ahead next time. A sign is also another way to let your community know that there is a new bed-and-breakfast in town. Even if your setting is somewhat remote and you can't envision much drive-by business, a sign is a helpful courtesy for first-time guests at your B&B. An attractive sign lends an air of professionalism to your establishment and will probably become a popular backdrop for guests' photos. Later, as they look through their photo album with friends and reminisce about their stay with you, the sign continues to advertise!

When you are ready to open for business, contact a features writer at your local town newspaper and see if you can persuade him or her to write an article about the newest B&B in town. A historic house is a good lure. Or perhaps you have some funny stories about the restoration. You should be able to find some angle that will spark their interest and convince them that the story is worth running. What is this publicity going to do for your business? For starters, it could help your standing in the community. This is always a plus, but especially so if you are a newcomer and your neighbors were less than enthusiastic about the idea of a B&B in *their* town. And you'd be surprised how many out-of-towners and out-of-staters continue to subscribe to their hometown newspaper—more potential business for you.

Contact local businesses and corporations and let them know that your bed-and-breakfast is conveniently located and well equipped to handle business travelers. If you have a large B&B, you could offer a corporate discount. It doesn't have to be much of a discount to help you nab more business. And business travelers are generally very easy to care for; they are up early, want a light breakfast, and then are off for the day.

To find out which advertising is working—and which isn't—get in the habit of asking callers how they got your phone number. Keep a record of this information.

Designing Your Business Card and Brochure

You will need business cards and brochures before you open your B&B for business. Unless you are artistically talented, you should work with a designer at a good print shop. As a guide and a source of ideas, use the brochures you've collected to do your rate research. As you'll find, the variety of brochures is almost mind-boggling. Some are single, narrow sheets the size of a business envelope, while others open to four panels and include color photographs. You will have to choose paper color and weight, ink color, and a layout design. Obviously, the more elaborate ones are more expensive to print. Since you will probably want to change your brochure within a year or two, and again over the years, it's wise not to make your first one too expensive. Decide on something that is a good and accurate reflection of you and your B&B, and have a small order printed. Five hundred is generally the minimum for a good price. The more you have printed, the less each one will cost you. Once all the graphic work and typesetting are done, the print shop should be able to quickly run off more for you as needed with just a phone call from you.

One of the biggest mistakes B&B hosts make when designing their brochures is exaggerating and overstating what they have to offer. You'll want to emphasize all that's special about your house, location, and amenities, but avoid building up the expectations of prospective guests to an unrealistically high level. You may know from firsthand experience how disappointing it is to arrive at your destination and find that the B&B you chose falls far short of its description in the brochure.

Your brochure should include a description of the house, inside and out, with particular emphasis on the guest rooms and baths. Be sure to include any historically or architecturally interesting information. State whether you serve a full or continental breakfast, and give a few appetizing details. Then you need to mention a little bit about what there is to see and do in your area. You should list rates or include a separate rate sheet; include directions from points north, south, east, and west (whatever applies); and mention any important restrictions at your B&B (such as, "We do not allow smoking inside the house") and state your policy on children. You should give your reservation/deposit/cancellation policy and check-in and check-out times. These are the basics. You can get into lots of details about all of these, depending on how much room you have in your brochure.

Whether your brochure is large or small, it's nice to include in it some kind of illustration. Line drawings can be much more evocative than photographs (and less expensive) and to my way of thinking are more in keeping with what bed-and-breakfasts are all about. If you can produce a good sketch of the outside of your house, that's wonderful. Otherwise it should not be hard to find a local artist who will do it, or look for an artist who advertises in the back of some of the trade publications, such as *The Inn Times*. Be sure to ask for samples of the artist's work in advance. The artist will ask you to send a photograph and will generally charge a set fee. If you have space for more than one sketch, perhaps one of a guest room, the dining room, or the porch would enhance the image you are trying to convey. Remember, your brochure is usually the first view of your B&B that your guests have.

Business cards are a little easier to design than brochures because there is a lot less to them. But there are still a lot of decisions to be made. Paper weight and color, ink color, and design are all considerations; all of these should match or somehow complement your brochure. Business cards that are actually photographs are becoming popular lately, and if that's your favorite, fine. But a word of advice: Often a photograph doesn't do justice to a place the way a line drawing can; colors can appear garish; and photographs can look dated quickly in a way that sketches don't.

If the name of your B&B doesn't indicate that the business *is* a bed-and-breakfast establishment, be sure to include that information somewhere on your card. For instance, if the name of your B&B is Lakeview and the only other information on the card is an address and phone number, it won't be immediately apparent that you're in the lodging business; Lakeview could be a restaurant, a campground, or a land development company. Because business cards are easily stored in wallets, while brochures are often misplaced or thrown away, they are often the survivors from a stop at a tourism information center. Make your business card one with some punch, so that when the person who stuck it in his wallet six months ago comes across it again, he doesn't wonder where in the world it's from—and what it's for—but will instead pick up the phone for more information or a reservation. As with brochures, a good minimum first order is usually a box of five hundred. Once the original artwork and typesetting are done, subsequent orders will be less expensive.

Stationery and Gift Certificates

Once you've been in business for a while, you'll probably want to have business stationery and gift certificates printed. Go back to the print shop that helped you with your brochure and business cards and work out a design for stationery that complements them. A gift certificate can take many forms; the print shop should be able to help you with ideas. You will want to include "To:" and "From:" lines, a description of what the certificate is good for (number of nights, single or double occupancy, dates it is valid, and any restrictions), a place for your signature, and some kind of illustration. If the gift certificate is going to be a different size from your business stationery, you'll need special envelopes as well.

Accepting Reservations

Learning how to take reservations properly is crucial to the success of your bed-and-breakfast. To do this, you will need to establish certain policies before opening for business, starting with how you'll answer the phone.

Most of your guests will call ahead to make reservations. You should get in the habit of answering the phone professionally, that is, by saying hello, followed by the name of your B&B, in a friendly voice. Be prepared to describe your bed-and-breakfast and area, to give rates, and to provide clear directions to your house. All that information will be in your brochure, but with some last-minute reservations you will not have time to mail one out, and most times callers want to confirm that information anyway before they make a reservation. Even though you will be saying the same things over and over, you'll need to sound fresh and enthusiastic for each caller. Imagine what you'd want to know if you were on the other end of the phone. Do more than simply provide answers to the questions posed; try to anticipate what callers might want to know and give them lots of information before they ask for it. If you sound professional, friendly, and interested, you are much more likely to get a reservation than the host who sounds lackluster, annoyed, or bored and who supplies one-word answers. Anyone else who will be answering the phone at your B&B should be trained to answer the phone properly, give information, and take reservations.

It is possible to "screen" prospective guests over the phone when they call to inquire about making a reservation. If the party on the other end is sounding too fussy, too grumpy, or too completely unfamiliar with what a bed-and-breakfast is all about and you're pretty sure they wouldn't be happy with yours, you always have the option of saying something like, "I'm glad you called, Mrs. Jones, but it sounds as though you may need to call a few other B&Bs before you're ready to decide on a reservation. Here are a few numbers for other B&Bs in the area I can recommend."

But be forewarned: some people who may sound like bad prospects over the phone may turn out to be your favorite guests. Although you'll be acting largely on your intuition, be careful not to turn away callers too quickly—you could end up missing out on some delightful guests.

When I had been in business only a couple of years, I was eager to accept just about any reservation I could get. One evening, after I was already in bed (not my favorite time to take reservation calls), a gentleman from New York City called to make a reservation. The entire time we were talking I could hear a woman in the background asking him to inquire about this and that, and giving him constant instructions about what to say in what sounded like a very strident tone. He had just about made the reservation when he asked me if I could hold on a moment while he talked with his wife, then came back on the line to say yes, they would take the room.

Back in bed I wondered why I had accepted a reservation from a couple who were probably going to be impossible to please and I awaited their arrival the next day with misgivings. They turned out to be wonderful people—fun, lively, and interesting company who *loved* my bed-and-breakfast, and over the course of the next couple of years came back many times. I learned later that all the questions on that first call were the result of an earlier unsatisfactory bed-and-breakfast stay. They loved this area so much they eventually moved here, and are now two of our favorite friends—real friends. They continue to send business my way, and her mother has an open invitation to stay here, as my guest, whenever she wants.

The lesson here is this: use the "let me help you find another B&B more to your liking" line sparingly. It may be a much bigger loss than the forfeited revenue.

If you have teenage children living at home, you may want to get separate phone lines. Or, especially if your B&B is going to be a large operation, you should have a business phone listing separate from your family phone number. That way it's easy to know if an incoming call is personal or business. For hosts with small B&Bs and no children at home, a single line is fine, but consider having call waiting added to your service; with call waiting you won't miss important business calls when you're on the phone with a friend. An answering machine is a must for your business. Compose a professional and welcoming statement inviting callers to leave a detailed message about their reservation inquiries, or to leave their address if they have called to request a brochure.

The Reservation Calendar

You will need a reservation calendar, which you should keep in a handy spot near the phone. Your reservation calendar should show an entire month at a time. It should have blocks or boxes for each day that are large enough to divide into spaces equal to the number of rooms you'll be renting, and each space should be large enough to write a few key words. If you will be renting out four rooms, for instance, each box should be large enough to divide into four sections, and you should be able to write the last name of the guests, the number of nights they will be staying, and the room reserved for them. The rest of the details will be on the reservation sheet you filled out when you took the reservation. If each room has a distinct color scheme, you can also make a mark with erasable colored pencils to indicate the room that is reserved, extending the color line through the entire length of the stay; that way, anyone looking at the calendar (including you!) can see at a glance which rooms are reserved. This technique can help you avoid overbooking. Use a pencil or an erasable pen on your reservation calendar, so that when there is a cancellation, you can erase the information.

Reservation Sheets

Along with the calendar, you'll need reservation sheets, which can be conveniently kept on a clipboard with a pencil. Your reservation sheet should look something like this:

Reservation

current date: _____

source: _____

Name: _____

Phone #: (home) _____

(business) _____

Address: _____

_____

Number of people in party: (adults) _____

(children/ages) _____

Room(s) reserved: _____

Date(s) of reservation: _____

(number of nights) _____

Room rate quoted: _____

Sending deposit of: _____

Form of payment: _____

Cancellation policy given: _____

Expected time of arrival: _____

Notes: _____

_____

_____

Always ask first-time callers how they got your number. Jot the answer down on your reservation sheet on the Source line; at the end of each season you can compile this information and see which advertising has been most worthwhile.

Once your callers have decided that your B&B sounds right for them, and you have determined (by checking your reservation calendar) that a room is available for the dates in question, you need to collect some important information from them.

After taking down their name, get their home and business phone numbers; you may need both. Next get a mailing address, where you'll be sending the written confirmation once you've received their deposit or immediately, if they are using a credit card. While the next item on the sheet (number of people in party) may seem silly, it isn't. For some odd reason, all too often callers won't bother to tell you that they will be bringing along not only their spouse but a child or two; it's as if the kids are invisible! When you get to this part of the sheet, you can say something like, "Fine, Mr. Smith, I've reserved the room with the queen-sized bed and private bath for you and your wife for three nights at ninety-five dollars per night. That's a room for the two of you; is that correct?" It is here you will find that a startling number of callers say, "Oh, well, we'll have our five-year-old with us too, but that's not a problem, is it?" You must clarify this point while you are on the phone in order to avoid unpleasant surprises at check-in time. If the reservation does include children, make a notation of how many there are in the party and their ages.

Next make a notation of the room or rooms that are being reserved. You may have a name for each room, as many B&Bs do, such as the quilt room, the tower room, or the garden suite, or you may have a color code for each room—the rose room, the blue room, and so on. It doesn't really matter as long as the system is easy and you use it consistently; anyone else referring to the reservation sheets should be able to tell at a glance which rooms are taken.

Repeat the dates the caller has asked for, including the day of the week, by saying something along the lines of, "I'm reserving the room with two twin beds for you, Mrs. Smith, for July twenty-seventh and twenty-eighth; that's a Tuesday and Wednesday night." It might seem silly to you now to think that you have to be this specific, but it is very important and can save you time and trouble later. Quite often callers will accidentally be looking at the wrong month on their calendar; by stating the dates *and* days, you are helping to alert them to any mistake on their part. If the caller really wanted to reserve a Monday and Tuesday, for instance, this is her chance to catch the error.

The number of nights is extremely important to clarify because most callers will say that they want to reserve "days," and when they refer to "two days," quite often they really mean one night. It is the number of nights that you need to know for your reservation calendar purposes. So when a prospective guest asks for a "two-day stay, Saturday and Sunday," you need to repeat back to him as you are filling out the reservation sheet, "All right, Mr. Smith, I'm reserving the suite with the king-sized bed and private bath for you and your wife for two nights, Saturday and Sunday; you'll be checking out Monday morning." This is where some callers will say, "Oh, no, we just need Saturday night."

Since you will probably have a range of rates, it's important to make a note of the rate quoted for each reservation. If you don't do this, and the deposit check in the amount of one hundred dollars arrives with no details, it may be difficult for you to remember if you quoted your highest rate of eighty-five dollars per night, or if you offered them a slightly reduced rate for some reason. You don't want to find yourself in the embarrassing and unprofessional position of having to ask your guests what you told them you were going to charge.

You will be discussing a deposit for each reservation, except for very last-minute ones. It is standard to require a 50 percent deposit, or payment in full for a one-night reservation. Some B&Bs require advance payment in full for any holiday weekend reservations. See what is commonly done at the B&Bs you frequent and the others in your area, and go with a policy that you feel most comfortable with. Make a note of the deposit that you have told the caller to send. If it is a last-minute reservation and the caller will not have time to mail you a deposit, be sure to mention if you are a B&B that does not accept credit cards. By informing callers ahead of time, you can avoid having guests who are unable to pay their bill.

If you accept credit cards, enter the credit card information—number, expiration date, and name that appears on the card—and make a note of the amount being charged to the account on the form of payment line.

This is a good time to mention briefly your cancellation policy, if the caller hasn't already asked. As you do, make a check mark on that line on the reservation sheet. If the party does cancel later (after you've received their deposit but before they've received your brochure, which will include this information), you will know that the caller *was* informed of your policy.

The next piece of information on the reservation sheet is extremely important, especially if your operation will be too small to have full-time staff. You will have told the caller when check-in begins, but you need to ask for an expected time of arrival. Ask the caller for an approximate time—a two-hour time frame is reasonable—and make a note of it. While making the note, repeat back to your caller that unless you hear otherwise, you will be expecting their party to arrive between those hours. If the caller asks why you need to know, say that you want to be sure you're home and not off grocery shopping when they ring the bell. Waiting for late guests to arrive is one of the most exasperating parts of this business, as you'll soon find out, and guests who arrive hours early only to find no one there to welcome them are often quite indignant. Stressing the importance of a predictable arrival time over the phone will help save you and your guests from starting off your introduction to one another on the wrong foot.

The next section of the reservation sheet is where you should put any general notes that could be important for you to know. Callers volunteer a great deal of information over the phone, such as, "That weekend will be our tenth wedding anniversary," "We're coming to town for the Law of the Sea conference," or "Our son will be competing in the junior golf tournament that weekend." Whatever information they give you should be noted, whether it's a honeymoon, birthday, friend's wedding, class reunion, or business seminar that will bring them to your door. When a caller doesn't give you any such information, ask, "What brings you to our town?" This friendly question can yield important details. Callers may then tell you that this will be their first bed-and-breakfast experience. It's good to make a note of this; you may want to go out of your way to make them feel welcome when they first arrive. Or if they mention that their friends (who have stayed at your B&B and loved it) referred them, make a note of this too. If a caller tells you while you are describing breakfast that he is a vegetarian, make a note of it. By now you should be getting the picture of what this part of the reservation sheet is for: the information you gather here will prepare you to cater to your guests' special circumstances.

You may think of other things you want to include on your reservation sheet. Once you have composed one that suits your business, type it up and have copies made. A box of 250 sheets is a good start. Inexpensive copy paper is fine for this purpose.

Keeping a Reservation File

Place the reservation sheets in a file divided into months with a manila folder for each day. Mark a tab on the top of each folder with the date, and place the reservation sheets in the folder for the first day of the reservation. Your file box will have a distinct separator for each month of the year or your season, clearly labeled, and within each month there will be thirty or thirty-one folders (except February), each one numbered in consecutive order. A reservation that begins on June 5, for instance, is placed in the folder marked 5 in the June file. These reservations should match your reservation calendar; make sure you cross-reference each one carefully as you file it.

Even with a complete reservation file, you need a calendar so that you can see at a glance when you have space available. Many calls will be for information only; with a calendar you can quickly tell prospective guests whether or not you have space for the dates they are interested in reserving. With these two systems kept up-to-date, you should not have any problems with accidental overbookings. But somehow overbooking happens to even the most organized hosts at least once.

What to Do When You Overbook

If you find as you are updating your files that you have overbooked a room, remedy the situation immediately. First make a few calls to see if any other B&B in your area (with rates and services similar to yours) has a room available for those dates. Try to come up with at least three alternatives. Then call the party whose reservation is most recent, explain your error, and offer them your apologies and the alternatives you have found. If you have already received a deposit, tell them you will return it to them in that day's mail.

If you don't discover an overbooked room until two parties check in for it, be polite, and honor the older of the two reservations. Then do whatever you can to satisfy the ousted party. Make phone calls for them until you find suitable accommodations, refund their deposit, and if they are still really steamed, consider offering them a one-night gift certificate, good for one year. This should help mend things in most cases.

There are times, however, when you may need to be even more inventive than this to handle an overbooking at your B&B—especially if your setting is remote, or if everyone else in the area is booked.

One hot July morning I was interrupted from cooking breakfast by a telephone call. On the other end was a guest I was expecting the following weekend, asking if she and her friend could check in early that day.

"Today? Aren't you arriving a week from today?" I asked.

"No, our reservation is for *this* weekend, I have the confirmation letter right here."

I didn't need to look at my calendar to know I was overbooked. The only new guests I expected that day was a couple coming to join another couple who had been staying at my B&B for the entire week. They had mentioned more than once how much they were looking forward to being joined by his sister and brother-in-law for the weekend.

I told the woman on the phone that I'd make some calls and try to find her something. This lovely woman had been coming to my B&B for four years, and when I made this suggestion she said she didn't want to stay anywhere else, and that something would work out; she was on her way and would see me in a couple of hours.

I already knew from conversations with other hosts and the people at the chamber of commerce during the week that there was not a single room to be had in town that weekend. There was nothing to do but prepare the master bedroom and bath (my husband's and my bedroom) for the soon-to-arrive sister and brother-in-law. Since I've only overbooked one other time in nine years, my husband was a good sport about it and helped me set up two cots for us in the basement, where there is also a bathroom.

As it turned out, that weekend was hotter than it had been in forty-one years in our state—it was truly a record-breaking heat wave. The basement was the coolest place in the house—so cool that we had to sleep with blankets. At the end of a long hot day, we lay in the cool cellar on our little cots with our feet hanging off the ends, and laughed out loud at our situation. It was so unlike what sleeping at home is usually like, we imagined we were away somewhere, maybe at summer camp, and talked and laughed the night away.

The couple that stayed in the master bedroom couldn't have been more pleased, and the weekend went well for all. Both couples have made plans to come back and are joking about who will get the master bedroom suite next time.

Sometimes what looks like an impossible situation in this business turns out to be a bonus—but you'll need to keep your sense of humor, and more important, have an understanding spouse.

There are computer software reservation programs designed for use in large B&Bs. Information on them can be found on page 186 in the appendix. Even if you opt for such a system, you'll need to keep a calendar, and you'll need to make and file a hard copy (printed page) of every reservation entered into your computer file. The system given above should work for most B&Bs, large or small.

Written Confirmations

Once you receive a deposit, you should send out a written confirmation of some sort. This can be a form letter that you have on a computer file, with blanks for the party's name, dates of stay, room rate, etc. Print one copy on your business stationery and one on cheap computer paper. Staple the copy to the back of the original reservation sheet, and make a notation at the top of the reservation sheet of the amount and date of the deposit received. Then sign the one on your stationery and mail it off with one of your brochures. (Surely you can now understand the reason for a processing fee when there is a cancellation!) Your guests will be reassured to see their reservation confirmed in writing, and you will have a thorough file that makes it easy to keep track of things—especially helpful when you reach that sought-after 100 percent occupancy.

Handling Check-in

Check-in, a crucial time for you and your guests, has two important elements for you to handle. First, you must make your guests feel welcome and at ease, and second, you'll need to collect any monies due on the reservation.

Once guests arrive at your B&B, you can proceed with check-in a couple of different ways. One option is to show guests to their room right away, telling them that you will meet them in the foyer (or living room, or wherever you keep your guest register and receipts) in ten minutes to settle the bill and show them around. This option gives them a chance to freshen up and do a little unpacking before taking care of the bill. Or you can greet guests at the door when they arrive and immediately direct them to the guest register.

Either way, have guests fill out and sign a ledger that has a place for date, name, home address, phone number, and driver's license. You should have already filled in the space that gives the length and dates of their stay. There are a large number of styles of registers to choose from; visit an office supply store and purchase one that suits you. Or design your own, print one, have copies made, and put them in a looseleaf binder.

While your guests are signing in, you can be making out the receipt for the balance due on their reservation, if they have sent you a deposit, or the entire amount, if they have not. If they are paying with a credit card, you will need to run the card through a validator, fill out the form, call the credit card company for an authorization number, and have the guest sign the form.

By taking care of payment when guests arrive, you can avoid some unpleasant situations that can arise when these details are not attended to right away, such as guests who decide to check out a day or two early because they don't like the weather (if they haven't already paid their total bill, you can be sure they won't); guests who as they are leaving realize that they have used up all the cash they had with them and have left their credit card/ATM card/checkbook at home (you may never collect on this one); and last-minute guests who innocently say after one night that you must have misunderstood them, they didn't want to reserve two nights, just one. By having your guests sign a register that indicates the dates of the reservation and collecting any monies due before you give them a house key or room key, you will eliminate any possible confusion later. This policy will also allow you to enjoy your guests more readily, because you can concentrate on other aspects of your business without wondering if there will be some kind of problem when you present them with the bill for their stay.

Always give guests a receipt. You can purchase receipt books at stationery or office supply stores; buy one that has a large format with at least four receipts per page; the single-receipt-per-page style is more difficult to write on and you will run out faster. Be sure to keep extra receipt books on hand. Use a receipt book that makes carbonless copies; give one to your guest and staple your copy to their reservation sheet in your reservation file. The receipt copy, the final piece of information in your reservation file, will be important to your record keeping. Now you are ready to show your guests around, answer any questions they may have, and get on with your business while they get on with their vacation.

You should check guests in personally whenever possible, but on those occasions when you can't, your help should be competent to handle the procedure.

Checking guests in for the first time can be a little confusing, and you may be a bit nervous about it. Practice with a friend or family member, so that when your first guests arrive, you can handle the check-in with grace and confidence.

Reservation Services

There are a slew of B&B reservation agencies around the country now. Look in your yellow pages or call your state tourism department to find one for your area. Essentially, a B&B reservation agency will accept and arrange the reservations for your bed-and-breakfast (and many others in your region), deduct a commission for each booking (usually 20 percent), and mail you the balance. The services they provide, however, can be much more extensive, and for some B&Bs they are the main source of bookings. Although listing your business with a reservation service may not be right for you, there are a number of advantages to be considered.

If you have an isolated location, a reservation agency can help you establish a following much faster. If you don't want to have a B&B sign on your house, don't want any walk-up business, don't want to have brochures made, don't want to bother with advertising, don't want to be responsible for keeping a reservation calendar and file, and don't want to send written confirmations, then a reservation agency may be just the thing for you. The agency will essentially take care of all of these details for you.

The reservation agency will advertise your B&B for you in a publication of all their listings that they mail to interested parties. They also advertise in major B&B guidebooks, and, as mentioned, they are listed in the yellow pages under "Bed-and-Breakfast." The agency will call you to see if you can accept the reservation that a caller (on hold on another line) wants to make at your B&B. You can say yes or no; if you say yes, the agency will take all the information from the prospective guests, process the deposit and payment in full, send out the written confirmation, and give directions to your B&B. Because reservation agencies accept credit cards, there is never any problem with payment for last-minute bookings. Once a month, you will receive a check from the agency for all completed reservations. If you decide to let an agency handle all your bookings, you will have much more free time, which you can use to pursue another business or profession, at home or away.

Hosts whose B&Bs are listed with reservation agencies usually take some bookings directly on their own and get the balance from the service. As you can see, if you find a reservation service with which you are completely pleased, you could balance your bookings in whatever way is best for you.

Now that you've got a calendar full of bookings, all you have to do is wait for guests to arrive. Then the real fun begins.

9
The Art of
Hosting

> *W*hate'er he did was done
> with so much ease,
> In him alone, 'twas natural
> to please.
> —JOHN DRYDEN

Gracious Hospitality

*Y*our ability to be a gracious host will probably be the most important element in the success of your business. Yes, you must have clean, comfortable rooms, but even spectacular accommodations can be spoiled by sour hosts, just as homey ones are made special by genuine, generous hospitality. Your image as a gracious host begins when you answer the phone to accept a reservation, and it continues until you wave good-bye to departing guests.

Being a gracious host is an art, but it's one that you can learn if you have the desire. If you do your best to be warm, welcoming, and concerned about each guest's comfort, safety, and enjoyment, your guests will give back to you such gratitude and appreciation that your job will become easier and easier, as well as a lot more pleasant. Also, your B&B will become successful and thereby earn more money. If you are a reluctant host—grumpy, short-tempered, inflexible—your unhappy guests will make you the object of their displeasure. They will not shower you with compliments and smiles; they will be demanding and rude. They are unlikely to return or to send referral business your way.

What is hospitality, and how does one become good at it? It is making strangers feel welcome, making weary travelers feel refreshed, and making all your guests feel pampered and special. These pleasures can be conferred in many little ways: Greet your guests at the door with a smile and a warm greeting. Even if you don't provide afternoon tea at your bed-and-breakfast, offer each new arrival a drink—traveling induces thirst—something cold and icy if it's hot outside, or a pot of coffee or tea if it's cold or stormy. This simple gesture will mean a lot to your guests, and it doesn't take much time, effort, or expense on your part.

Once your guests have signed the register and paid, give them a brief tour, pointing out where breakfast will be served and which parts of the house and grounds they are welcome to use and asking them if they have any questions. This attention will give you a chance to get to know them a bit and will help them start to feel at home. This is also a good time for you to find out what may be of particular interest to them while they are in the area. With this information, you can point them toward some special places that they might otherwise have missed. All of these little things will let your guests know that you care and are there to help them get the most out of their visit.

Get Organized

Probably the single most important thing you can do as you begin your apprenticeship in the art of gracious hospitality is to get organized. Running a bed-and-breakfast requires so many different skills—cooking, cleaning, laundering, booking reservations, filing, and accounting—all while you attempt to create an ambiance of a beautiful and special place, that if you are not well organized you can quickly become frazzled. Once you start to feel frazzled, you will begin to lose that pleasant manner that you usually have in social situations. Here is where a big misconception about this job comes in: if you thought that being a good host meant putting on your best smile and settling in for a long chat with your guests, think again! Your guests will want to chat with you (often when you don't have the time or inclination to chat!), but if you are organized, keeping an even disposition while you deal with the many and varied demands of guests will be much easier. The better organized you are, the more relaxed and available for pleasant conversation you will be.

If you've been paying attention to the tips and guidelines given in previous chapters, you've already made a good start in that direction. Your linen closet is well ordered and supplied; cleaning items and equipment for the guest rooms, bathrooms, and the rest of the house are together in one convenient place, with plenty of extra supplies on hand; your reservation system is thorough, organized, and up-to-date; and your pantry is well stocked with breakfast staples. Your house rules, carefully thought

out, are clearly stated in each guest room; your brochure and business cards are designed to present an inviting and accurate image of your B&B; and your sensible rates, discounts, and cancellation policies are in writing. All necessary licenses and permits have been obtained and are attractively framed and on display, your insurance policy covers your home and B&B business completely, and you have joined the local chamber of commerce or bed-and-breakfast host association. You have trained competent and reliable helpers. All of these steps take time and money, but following them will put you in a position to succeed in this business and will greatly help you to be a gracious host.

The Privacy Factor

In addition to these very tangible basics, there are a number of other, more obscure, things you can do to help ensure that you maintain your composure and that your guests view you as a superb host. Before you open for business, make sure that you have set aside a part of the house and yard as a private place for you and your family. Being able to get away from your business and spend time with your spouse or children without the inter- ruptions of guests will restore your spirits and keep you fresh.

Just as you'll need your privacy, guests want some from you too. Don't hover. Don't make the mistake of feeling compelled to stop and chat with guests every time you pass them coming and going. You not only will be wearing yourself out, but may be tiring them out as well. You don't want them to rush off to their room whispering under their breath, "I thought she'd never stop talking! I thought she'd never leave us alone!" Guests will want to get to know you, but they also want some time alone with each other. The weekend at your B&B may be the first vacation or time away from kids they've had in years.

Hired Help

Determine whether you'll need part-time or full-time help and make the necessary arrangements. Your own teenage children are probably *not* the best helpers for your business; they may resent the B&B and be rude to guests. And you don't want to be arguing with your child about a poorly cleaned bathroom when new guests arrive. It's better to run an ad in your local paper and to interview respondents carefully. Once you've found someone dependable with the proper skills, be sure to employ the person for more than just manual chores. Allow your help to check in guests and answer the phone so that you can get to your watercolor class, tennis game, gardening club, or any other important activity. The dream of working at home can become a nightmare if you are never able to get out for a change of scene. Being able to keep up with outside interests will help you present your best self to guests.

Train your help to do all the chores that need to be done to run the B&B, even though you plan on being there each day. There will be times when you are ill and unable to prepare the breakfast; there will be family emergencies that take you away from home; and there will be special events like weddings that you won't want to miss just because you have a full house.

Be a Guest

Plan a few getaways every year that include B&B stays. If you have excellent help, you can go away during your business season; if your operation is open year-round, getaways are a must. If your business is seasonal, you'll have an easier time planning vacations during the off season, but I recommend that you still try to get out for at least a two- or three-day break during your busy time. These little vacations can do a lot for you. For one thing, they will provide you with some much-needed rest and relaxation. Staying at other B&Bs is educational; you'll get new ideas about how to improve things at your own place. And when you get home, you'll have a fresh perspective on how you're doing and, just as important, what it's like to be a guest. Traveling is usually a lot of fun, but it's tiring too, and hosts need to be reminded of the guests' point of view.

Become a Member

Be sure to attend the meetings of your local B&B association, though it's easy to find excuses why you're too busy that evening. If there isn't a local organization, get together with a few of the other area hosts and see if you can get one going. These groups can be a terrific help, especially to the new host. Meetings are a time to share stories—good and bad—let off steam, and have a few laughs. But they're also a good way to share business tips and keep up with the latest changes in the local B&B scene. Hosts usually take turns hosting a meeting, and this is a good way to see the other B&Bs so that you'll know whether you want to recommend them when you are full. You'll also want to take advantage of all the referral business that established hosts can send your way if your B&B is up to snuff.

Honesty

Offer what you advertise. As mentioned earlier, there is nothing to be gained by exaggerating your house, guest rooms, or breakfast. Guests will be disappointed, at the least, or even downright angry. This kind of reaction will not help you as a host. It's much better to advertise what is best about your B&B in a simple, truthful way. Chances are, guests *are* going to love your place, but they'll marvel over their good fortune at finding you if you've understated all that's special at your bed-and-breakfast.

Attention to Detail

There are many other little things you can do that will help visitors enjoy their stay at your B&B:

- Collect menus from local restaurants and put them in a looseleaf binder for guests.
- Type up directions from your B&B to the most popular points of interest in your area. Have copies made and keep a good supply on hand.
- Collect from your state and local tourism board all the free maps and brochures they publish for visitors. Keep these attractively displayed for guests to take as they please.
- Keep on hand any discount coupons you can find for admissions to local events and share these with guests.

All of these little extras will seem like thoughtful touches to your guests, but they are a great help to you too. Guests at your B&B *will* want restaurant recommendations, suggestions for day trips, and directions. If you supply them with all of this information in advance, they are more likely to choose something that suits their taste, and you are spared repeating the same information thousands of times. The host who must constantly repeat the same directions over and over or the host whose own dinner is frequently interrupted by requests for restaurant suggestions is going to get annoyed with guests who are really perfectly nice people. When this happens, gracious hospitality starts to slip.

Above and Beyond

Be prepared occasionally to do some things for your guests that will be outside the realm of your regular hosting duties. Here's an example of what I mean: Last year an expected couple arrived at my doorstep much later than they had advised me, looking exhausted and worried. They had left their home in California early that morning and spent the entire day in transit. Flights had been delayed, connections missed, and to top it all off, their luggage had been lost. They had taken no carry-on bags, so they had absolutely nothing but the clothes on their backs. The airline assured them that the luggage had been located and would be delivered to them that evening by courier. As I commiserated with them about the state of flying today, I fixed them up with some tea. Later, while they were out having dinner, the airline called to say that the bags would be delivered the next morning, not that evening. I could have simply left a note with that information in their room, knowing that they would then want to know where they could purchase some toiletries, at the least. Having done a lot of traveling myself, I could imagine what an unhappy prospect that would be, so I left them the note along with two new, still-in-the-box toothbrushes, a tube of toothpaste, a new razor and shaving cream for the gentleman, and a freshly laundered nightgown for the woman. This very small gesture meant so much to them that when I saw them at breakfast the next morning, they couldn't stop thanking me. While they were eating, their luggage *did* arrive, and the rest of their vacation was saved. If you can give of yourself in this way, your guests will consider you the ultimate host.

Dealing with Unpleasant Guests

You will, sooner or later, have to deal with unpleasant guests. These are people who are rude, thoughtless, selfish, or snobbish. Fortunately, there aren't many of these types among B&B enthusiasts, but when you get some staying under your roof, they may rankle you. There are ways to lessen the irritation. If you've properly made a schedule for yourself that allows you some time away from the business each day, use this time to complain about them, laugh about them, and get them out of your system.

Remind yourself that their stay is limited; they haven't moved in with you permanently. Better still, try to view them with some sympathy. Perhaps they have a very unsatisfactory personal life, perhaps they've just received some bad news at work, or perhaps they are actually a little jealous of all that you appear to have. Keeping these thoughts in mind, try to go out of your way to offer these sour sorts a little extra warmth; you may just be pleasantly surprised at the results. Even if you aren't, remaining your best self in the face of their rudeness will leave you feeling better during their stay and after they leave. If you let one unpleasant guest upset you, it will be hard to hide that from other guests; you will either be making *them* uncomfortable at seeing your anger, or worse, you'll be short-tempered with them too. We all have our flaws. It shouldn't be too hard for you to remind yourself of your own and to judge your "bad" guests a bit less harshly.

Enjoy Yourself

As a bed-and-breakfast host, you have a unique opportunity to meet people from around the world. Give yourself a chance to get to know a little bit about each one; you'll find these strangers touch your life in ways you would never have imagined possible. Each guest brings some small life story with them that is enriching and educational—even inspiring.

Don't make assumptions about your guests, and don't underestimate them. Learn to be a listener. Allow yourself to enjoy the guests in this unique business; when your guests see your pleasure, they will enjoy themselves more too. As the years go by, you'll derive great satisfaction and a sense of accomplishment as you read the entries in your guest book. You'll remember faces and personalities and snippets of conversation as you read the names and addresses from around the globe. And if you're doing things right, most of the comments will include notes like, "Thank you so much for everything! We can't wait to come back and see you again!" Yes, *you* will be the reason they return. You, the gracious host.

10

Staying in Business

To business that we love
we rise betime,
And go to 't with delight.
—William Shakespeare

You're in Business!

*A*fter a lot of work getting your house and rooms ready and permits and licenses in order, and getting the word out that your bed-and-breakfast is open for business, you must now master the intricacies of staying in business.

Bookkeeping

The first matter of concern for most new hosts is income—how to turn a profit. Start by keeping good records of all business income and expenses. Save every receipt and start a filing system strictly for your B&B business. If your B&B is going to be a large operation—more than two spare bedrooms—consider starting a separate business checking account; this makes it even easier to keep track of income and expenses.

Whether or not you decide to start a separate checking account, switch to a business-style check writing system. These are sheets of checks that come with large ledger pages that hold thirty-six checks at a time and allow you to itemize over forty categories, such as food, bedding, hired help, insurance, and cleaning supplies. Each check has a carbon line running through it so that the information is automatically recorded on the ledger page as you fill in the check. With this kind of system, you can ascertain at a glance how much you are spending on your business overall and on individual expenses. You will be able to determine where you are going wrong if you are running in the red, and the record will be of immense help to you and your accountant at tax time.

When you look at the records of the reservations during your first season in business, you'll need to decide if your rates are high enough (or too high) and if there are ways you could increase your business—and income. If you notice, for example, that on the weekends your B&B rooms are consistently completely full and you are turning callers away, consider a slight increase in your weekend rates. You should continue to experience full occupancy and will be increasing your profits. If you notice, on the other hand, that your calendar is largely blank during midweek, consider offering slightly lower rates to callers.

Tax Advantages

In addition to real income, your B&B should provide you with some savings at tax time. As your accountant will tell you, part of your home-owner's insurance, part of your property taxes, and part of your utility bills will all become business expenses and therefore tax deductions. Major renovations to the house, such as interior and exterior painting, new roof, new windows, or new furnace, can be deducted partially or in full. The costs of decorating guest bedrooms and outfitting guest bathrooms are business expenses. So if you were planning on restoring an old house anyway and like the idea of running a bed-and-breakfast for a few years, your business can help pay for the restoration in more ways than one. Even if you've always done your income tax return yourself, now that you own a business, you should enlist the help of a professional. Call around until you find a CPA who is familiar with bed-and-breakfast businesses. Nowadays that shouldn't be difficult.

Whether or Not to Incorporate

It's a good idea to sit down with an accountant before you open your B&B to discuss a number of things about your business, including for which employees, if any, you are required to pay social security tax and other state and local employment taxes. Your accountant will advise you on tax deductions, record-keeping ideas, and whether or not incorporating your business will be worthwhile from a financial point of view. Setting up a corporation is expensive; there are start-up accounting and legal costs, as well as annual fees and related taxes. The corporation may or may not increase the tax deductions and savings you can look forward to when you own your own business. The expense may only be justified if your bed-and-breakfast is going to be a large business, your primary source of income. Each situation is unique, so you will have to consider carefully all the options with a knowledgeable accountant.

Most people consider incorporating their businesses to limit their personal liability in the event of a claim. This is a matter to discuss with your lawyer. A corporation can add some protection but is not fail-safe, so if that is your only reason for incorporating, the step may not really be necessary. You are going to need a business insurance policy; perhaps that will be sufficient. Let your lawyer help you decide.

Making Money

The real secret to making money in this business is simple: you'll need to take in more than you spend. One way to guarantee a profit is not to overspend when you first open for business. You may be tempted to break your budget making your house perfect, but this is a mistake. Have patience; the business will help pay for continued renovations and finishing touches soon enough. If you spend more than you can honestly afford before you are making any money from your B&B, you are almost certain to fail. I read in one of the trade publications not long ago of a couple who completely renovated an enormous old house at great expense before opening for business. Having both left their jobs, they quickly depleted their cash reserves. Because they had overestimated what their B&B income would be, they eventually had to declare bankruptcy. From what I know of the situation, they could have avoided bankruptcy by spending less on start-up expenses. Their business was fairly busy, but they had incurred such large initial expenses that they just couldn't catch up. Don't make this mistake.

As suggested earlier, if you are starting your B&B with a partner or spouse, it's a good idea for one of you to continue working in your old job. The income will greatly aid you in surviving your first season and can allow you gradually to build a thriving business.

Spin-off Businesses

Even if your partner is continuing to bring in a regular paycheck, consider what other ways you could earn money while working at home running your B&B. You will probably have the time, since it will take a year or two to build a following, and if you've started another enterprise on the side while your B&B is slow, you'll probably find a way to keep it going even once your B&B business is booming. A number of hosts I know or have read about run busy B&Bs and still manage to run other home-based businesses—catering, desktop publishing, and landscape design, to name a diverse few. This other income can help you through the lean times and may actually turn out to be lucrative enough to carry the bed-and-breakfast! The most stunning example I know is that of a bed-and-breakfast in New England that was run by a woman who designed and made hand-hooked rugs, which she sold to her guests and other clients. Her bed-and-breakfast did well, but her rug business did even better, and she eventually closed the B&B to devote herself full-time to what had become a booming, internationally known, million-dollar business. This is an unusual case, but perhaps your bed-and-breakfast will allow you to turn another interest of yours into a profitable venture. It would be a shame not to try at least, now that you are at home working for yourself. Just remember, start *small*; that's what most successful businesses have done.

There may be a couple of things that you are going to be doing expressly for your bed-and-breakfast that are actually ways to make a little extra income from outside sources as well. For instance, if you have planted a good-sized cutting garden so that you can supply your guest rooms with your own fresh and dried flower arrangements all year, you will probably find that it is nearly impossible to use all the flowers you grow. Unless you live in the middle of nowhere, you should be able to find businesses that will gladly buy cut flowers from you, and not even arranged, just in jars of water; specialty produce markets, gourmet shops, and small restaurants are good places to start. The sideline won't make you rich, but every week those extra flowers could bring you fifty to a hundred dollars.

A similar way to let your bed-and-breakfast help you make some extra money is with baked goods. If you're a talented baker and are going to be baking batches of coffee cakes, quick breads, yeasted sweet rolls, and the like for your B&B anyway, why not make a bit more than you need? Local cafés, gourmet markets, and small restaurants may be interested in a regular supply.

Use your imagination. If you're energetic enough to run a B&B and are looking for another source of income without leaving home, chances are you'll be able to think of something!

The Horse's Mouth

What better way to find out how you're doing in business than to ask your customers? Design or purchase an attractive box and label it "Sug-

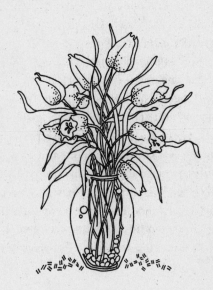

gestions." Place it on a hallway table where it is obvious to your guests and keep a pencil and a stack of index cards or a notepad next to it. Once a week or once a month go through it. The suggestions could be valuable in improving your business and making it a success.

Keep Guests Coming Back

You will gradually collect a substantial mailing list from your reservation file. You can encourage former guests to return for another visit by sending out newsletters. Depending on the size of your operation, do a mailing either four times a year at the changes of season or once a year (Christmas or New Year's is a good time). Compose a form letter (you can personalize each one as you stuff envelopes) in which, after a few pleasantries, you mention any improvements you've made to the B&B in the past year; any new and noteworthy happenings in your town; upcoming cultural events; interesting business, art, or craft seminars available in the area; and any special discounted rates you will be offering. Your guests will be touched that you remembered them, and you will undoubtedly get some bookings as a result. If you notice that certain newsletters were more successful than others in producing business, you've got more information on what is most interesting to your clientele.

If you have just a few rooms, you may be thinking that a newsletter isn't worth your time and effort. Get together with other small, local B&Bs (they'll be looking for creative ways to increase business in the off season too), and see if as a group you can come up with some appealing ideas. For instance, if one of the hosts is a quilter and another is an excellent baker, put together an off-season package that includes an afternoon of quilting instruction and another of baking lessons. If a group of you go in on offering your rooms at a discount for this package, with one host acting as the central reservation board, you could all end up profiting. Not only will you be filling rooms during a time of year when they might otherwise be empty, but you'll be attracting new business as well when former guests bring along newcomers. There are many different kinds of packages you can put together, depending on where you live. Be creative. You're in business for yourself now, so *you* have to find ways to make a paycheck.

Success

Large enterprise or small, succeeding in this business will be a bit of a juggling act. But if owning and running a bed-and-breakfast is your dream, you can make it work with a little planning and hard work. Use the tips and ideas in this book to get started. The challenges you'll face are what make the business so interesting and what will bring you your greatest satisfaction when your bed-and-breakfast succeeds.

Appendix: Resources

Bed-and-Breakfast Organizations

With one exception, these are national organizations. Membership will provide your business with added credibility and will provide you with a wealth of helpful information on industry standards, marketing and promotion, and the myriad details of successful bed-and-breakfast operations. You will become part of a network of B&B hosts, all hoping to share information and improve their businesses.

The National Bed & Breakfast Association
P.O. Box 332
Norwalk, CT 06852
(203) 847-6196

Professional Association of Innkeepers International
P.O. Box 90710
Santa Barbara, CA 93190
(805) 569-1853

The American Bed & Breakfast Association
1407 Huguenot Road
Midlothian, VA 23113
(804) 379-2222

New England Innkeepers Association
P.O. Box 1089
North Hampton, NH 03862
(603) 964-6689

Bed-and-Breakfast Reservation Agencies

This agency is the only nationwide reservation agency in the country. As a new bed-and-breakfast owner, you may be wise to join it; use the yellow pages of your telephone directory to find listings of smaller bed-and-breakfast reservation agencies for your city, state, or region (look under "Bed-and-Breakfasts," "Inns," or "Lodging").

Bed & Breakfast Reservation Center Nationwide
P.O. Box 6806
Bloomington, IN 47407
(800) 388-4403

Trade Publications

You'll want to request a sample issue of each before subscribing. These publications contain a wealth of timely articles, interviews, and advertisements for products and services directly related to the business. There is also a good classified section in each that lists for sale operating bed-and-breakfasts from around the country.

Inn Business Review
105 East Court Street
P.O. Box 1789
Kankakee, IL 60901
(815) 939-3509

The Inn Times
Suite 246
2101 Crystal Plaza Arcade
Arlington, VA 22202
(202) 363-9305

The Bed & Breakfast Locator
P.O. Box 471006
Fort Worth, TX 76147
(800) 327-7359

Guidebooks

Any of these will provide your B&B with good exposure. As you'll see, some target very specific markets. Do some research to find out which ones will work for you. You'll also want to visit your favorite bookstore to do some looking. When you find a guidebook that you like, write to the publisher to find out how to get your B&B listed in the next edition.

*B&Bs and Country Inns: The Complete Guide to Bed & Breakfasts
    and Country Inns*
P.O. Box 1355
Boston, MA 02205
(603) 433-8735

Bed & Breakfast in New England
Globe Pequot Press
138 West Main Street, Box Q
Chester, CT 06412

Bed & Breakfast in the Mid-Atlantic States
Globe Pequot Press
138 West Main Street, Box Q
Chester, CT 06412

Wakeman & Costine's North American Bed & Breakfast Directory
P.O. Box 6958
Lakeland, FL 33807
(800) 284-7798

National Trust Guide to Historic Bed & Breakfasts, Inns, and Small Hotels
1785 Massachusetts Avenue, NW
Washington, DC 20036
(202) 673-4000

The Annual Directory of American Bed & Breakfasts
513 Third Avenue South
Nashville, TN 37210
(615) 244-2700

The Original Bed and Breakfast Discount Directory
3 Cedar Street
Fair Haven, VT 05743
(802) 265-3160

The Official Bed and Breakfast Guide for the United States, Canada, Bermuda,
   Puerto Rico & U.S. Virgin Islands
P.O. Box 332
Norwalk, CT 06852
(203) 847-6196

American Historic Inns
P.O. Box 336
Dana Point, CA 92629
(714) 499-8070

The Non-Smoker's Guide to Bed & Breakfasts
513 Third Avenue South
Nashville, TN 37210
(615) 244-2700

At Your Service
737 E. 121 Terrace
Kansas City, MO 64146
(816) 942-5080

The Christian Bed & Breakfast Directory
P.O. Box 719
Uhrichsville, OH 44683
(914) 922-6045

Bed & Breakfast Guest Houses & Inns of America
P.O. Box 38066
Memphis, TN 38183
(901) 755-9613

Breakfast 'n Bed
1100 E. Hector Street, Suite 415
Conshohocken, PA 19428
(215) 941-0335

Resource Publications for the B&B Host

Here is one excellent magazine, three general resource books, and one cookbook for the bed-and-breakfast host. You may want to advertise in *Country Inns/Bed & Breakfast*.

Country Inns/Bed & Breakfast
P.O. Box 182
South Orange, NJ 07079
(800) 435-0715

Inn Business Yellow Pages
P.O. Box 1789
Kankakee, IL 60901
(815) 939-3509

Innovations
118 South Avenue E
Cranford, NJ 07016
(908) 272-3600

Guide to the Inn Guidebooks
Professional Association of Innkeepers International
P.O. Box 90710
Santa Barbara, CA 93190
(805) 569-1853

The Bed & Breakfast Cookbook
Stemmer House Publishers
2627 Caves Road
Owings Mills, MD 21117
(800) 345-6665

Reservation Software

If you want to keep your reservation system in your home computer, here are two popular programs to investigate.

InnSoft InnKeeper
(800) 288-2773

MacInn
(800) 755-9887

Insurance Companies

Your current homeowner's insurance policy will not be sufficient when you are running your B&B. Talk to your insurance agent, and get information from some of these companies as well.

Inn*Surance
Martinsburg, WV
(800) 825-4667

James W. Wolf, Insurance
Bed & Breakfast/Country Inns Insurance Program
P.O. Box 510
Ellicott City, MD 21041
(800) 488-1135

Bed & Breakfast Insurance Specialists
P.O. Box 65788
Salt Lake City, UT 84165
(800) 356-6517

Brown, Schuck, Townshend & Associates
6011 Executive Boulevard, Suite 205
Rockville, MD 20852
(800) 638-8561

Mail Order Catalogues

It's hard to leave home when your B&B gets busy, so here are some good catalogues with helpful products. Consider bulk orders with other B&Bs for discounts.

TOILETRIES

Travel Mates America
1760 Lakeview Road
Cleveland, OH 44112
(800) 284-7357

RENOVATION AND DECORATING

Country Curtains
Stockbridge, MA 01262
(800) 456-0321

Finishing Touches
306 Dartmouth Street
Boston, MA 02116
(800) 468-2240

Hold Everything
Williams-Sonoma
P.O. Box 7456
San Francisco, CA 94120
(800) 541-2233

Home Decorators Collection
2025 Concourse Drive
St. Louis, MO 63146
(800) 245-2217

Kemp & George
301 Madison Road
P.O. Box 511
Orange, VA 22960
(800) 456-0788

Renovator's Supply
Millers Falls, MA 01349
(800) 659-2211

Rue de France
Thames Avenue
Newport, RI 02840
(800) 777-0998

KITCHEN AND DINING ROOM

Calico Industries, Inc.
P.O. Box 2005
Annapolis Junction, MD 20701-2005
(800) 638-0828

A Catalogue for Cooks
Williams-Sonoma
P.O. Box 7456
San Francisco, CA 94120
(800) 541-2233

LINENS

The Company Store
500 Company Store Road
La Crosse, WI 54601
(800) 323-8000

Cuddledown of Maine
312 Canco Road
Portland, ME 04103
(800) 323-6793

Rue de France
Thames Avenue
Newport, RI 02840
(800) 777-0998

Schweitzer Linen
457 Columbus Avenue
New York, NY 10024
(800) 554-6367

Index

Entries in *italics* refer to recipes

Accountant, 35, 174, 175
Advertising, 11, 19, 24–25, 72, 136–40
    free, 139–40
Air freshener, 70
Alcohol, 125–26
Amenities, and rates, 132
Answering machine, 145
Apron, 99
Armchairs, 79
Armoires, 29, 46
Arrival time, expected, 149
Artwork, 50, 80
Aspirin, 124

Baked Eggs with Herbs and Cheese, 105
Baked goods, selling, 177
Baked Pears Hersey, 108–9
Balconies, private, 132

Barter, 53–54
Bath mat, 69, 73
Bathroom(s), 59–73
    accessibility, 55
    adding, 29–30, 37, 60, 64
    and breakfast seatings, 94
    cleanliness, 63
    etiquette, 60–62
    extras, 71–72
    renovation, 18–19
    necessities for, 60–63, 65–71
    number and location of, 60, 64
    private, 29–30, 52, 59–60, 63, 132
    safety, 124
    semiprivate, 63–64
    shared, 29–30, 47–48, 52, 59–64, 70, 94
Bath soap, 11
Bath towels, 19, 73

Bed-and-breakfast
  associations, 27–28, 163–64
  business side of, 9–13, 173–79
  buying existing, 18, 34–36
  daydream, vs. reality, 3–4
  defined, 4–6
  house, decor, and food, 7–9
  house for, 23–34
  as job, 10
  misconceptions about, 10–13
  organizations, 183–82
  pluses and minuses of, 13–15
  resource publications for, 185–86
  starting, xv–xvii
  start-up costs, 18–19, 31, 175–76
  staying at other, 163
  turning current house into, 36–37
  why decide to run, 15–17
Bed & Breakfast Cookbook, The (Murphy),
  102, 186
Bedding, 19, 43–45
  minimum needed, 45
Bedrooms or guest rooms, 41–55
  cost of preparing, 53–54
  extras, 49–51
  decorating, 51–54
  locks, 124
  necessities of, 41–49
  number, size and design of, 28–29
  and rates, 132
  and tax deductions, 174
Bedroom door, 51
Beds, 19
  making, 54
  quality, 42
  size, 28
Bedside tables, 44
Bedspreads, 43, 44, 45, 52
Bells B&B, The, 107
Biscuits, Buttermilk, 104
Birders, 95
Blankets, 43–44, 45
Bookkeeping, 7, 173–74

Bookshelves, 80
Box springs, 11, 42
Breakfast, 6, 8–9, 91–108
  in bed, 96–98
  and brochure, 141
  eating, with guests, 99–100
  how to serve, 98–99
  menus and recipes, 100–108
  options, 92–93
  and rates, 93, 132
  seatings, 94
  time, 11–12, 93–95
  where to serve, 96
Bridal shops, 139
Brochures, 11, 19, 25, 49, 72, 122, 152,
  162
  designing, 141
  where to put, 139–40
Brown, H. Jackson, Jr., 53
Brunch, 92
Buffet, 95
Bulletin boards, 139
Bureau, 44
Business cards, 11, 19, 162
  designing, 141, 142
Business management, 173–79
Business travelers, 24
  advertising for, 140
  breakfast for, 95
  meeting needs of, 86
  and rates, 134
Butter, 91
Buttermilk Biscuits, 104

Call waiting, 145
Cancellation and refund policy, 121, 162
  and taking reservations, 148–49
Carpeting, 47
Chamber of commerce, 24, 136–37
Check-in
  handling, 152–54
  time, 121–22, 149
Checking account, 173–74

Check-out time, 115
Checks, personal, 121
Check writing system, 173–74
Chest of drawers, 44
Children
 and brochure, 141
 and family rates, 134–35
 guests with, 29, 80
 and reservations, 147
 rules about, 118–20
 sharing room with parent, 135
 and suites, 51
 your own, 16, 30–31, 77, 78, 162–63
China, 19
Cleaning supplies, 11, 55, 72, 161
Cleanliness, 52, 53
 importance of, 54–55, 72
 of living room, 78, 80
 of shared bathroom, 63, 72
Clocks, 47
Closets, 29, 46, 52, 54
 for cleaning supplies, 55
 linen, 161
Coffee, 91–92, 94, 95, 99
Colleges or universities, 23–24, 30, 139–40
Colors, 52–53
Comforters, 43, 45
Common or public rooms, 30, 77–87
 number of, 81–82
 and rates, 132
Competitiveness, 136
Computer software reservation programs, 152, 186
Condiments, 85
Conference room, 86
Confirmations, 7
 sending written, 152
Continental breakfasts, 92, 93
 defined, 92
 and rates, 132, 135
 supplies for, 101
 time for, 95
Continental-plus breakfast, 92

Cooking tips, 100
Corian, 66
Cosmetic work, 32, 37
Couches, 79, 80
Country Inns/Bed & Breakfast magazine, 138, 185
CPR, 126
Credit cards
 payment procedure, 153
 and taking reservations, 148
 whether to take, 120, 135
Cups, bathroom, 69
Curb appeal, 25–26, 37
Curfew, 115
Curtains, 52, 53
Cutlery, 19

Day trip suggestions, 165
Decaffeinated coffee, 102
Decks, 82
Decor. *See* Furnishing and decor
Deposits, 121
 and taking reservation, 148
Detail, 164–65
Dietary restrictions, 94, 102
Dining room, 31, 94, 96
Directions, 164, 165
Discount coupons, for local attractions, 164
Discounts, 134–35, 162
 for business travelers, 140
Dogs, 84, 126. *See also* Pets
Don'ts
 for bathroom, 60
 for bedroom, 51–52
Double beds, 42, 44
Double-occupancy rooms, 42
Drapes and curtains, 46, 54, 80, 81
Dresser, 44
Drug allergies, 124
Dusting, 54
Dust ruffles, 43, 45, 53
Duvet covers, 45

Eating with guests, 99–100
Eggs, Baked, with Herbs and Cheese, 105
Electrical outlets, 47–48
    bathroom, 66, 124
Electrical system, 32
Emergency exits, 55
Envelopes, 11
Expenses, 11
    deductible, 16–17, 174
    keeping down, 175–76
    operating, 18, 29
    of preparing guest rooms, 53–54
    and record keeping, 173
    start-up, 18–19

Families
    and bathrooms, 64
    discounts, 134–35
    See also Children
Family, your own
    and bathroom, 60
    emergencies, 163
    living room, 78, 82
Fans, 49
Fax machine, 86
Fiberglass showers, 67
Fire exits, 55
Fire inspection, 122–23
Fireplace, 81, 132
Fire safety, 118, 122–23
    and smoking, 114
Flashlight, 44
Floor, washing, 54, 63
Flowers, 11, 98
Food
    allergies, 125
    costs, 11
Footboards, 42
Full breakfasts
    defined, 92
    and rates, 93, 132
    supplies, 101
    time for, 94, 95

Furnishings and decor, 8, 52, 98, 174
    bedrooms, 30, 52–54
    living room, 80–81, 82
    porch, 83
Future bookings and deposits, 35. *See also*
    Reservations

Garden, 176–77
GFI outlets, 66, 124
Gift certificates, 143, 151
Glassware, 19
Grill, 84–85
Guest book, 98
Guest ledger or register, 153
Guests
    enjoying, 167–68
    items left behind by, 54
    and location type, 24–25
    satisfaction, 35
    screening, 144
    socializing with, 10
    uninvited, of B&B guests, 116–17
    unpleasant, rude, 11–13, 166–67
Guidebooks, 183–85
    listings, 137

Hair dryers, 48, 61
Half bath, available to guests, 62
Hand towels, 62
Hangers, 46, 52
Headboard, 42
Health insurance, 15, 17
Heat and air conditioning costs, 11
    and rates, 133
Heating system, 32, 37
Hersey House B&B, 107
Hired help, 7, 11, 16
    checklist for, 55, 72
    and hospitality, 162–63
    number of rooms and need for, 28–
        29
    and taxes, 175
    training, 55

Holiday rates, 133
Honesty, 164
Hospitality
    defined, 160
    and extras, 166
    and organization, 160–62
Hosts and hosting
    art of, 159–68
    defined, 6–7
    responsibilities of, 7, 9
Hot water, 67
    costs, 11
    heater, 32, 37
House
    appeal of, 25–26
    condition of, 32, 37
    layout and design of, 28–34, 37, 60
    location of, 23–25
    and zoning, 26–28
Housekeeping, 54–55
House rules, 113–27, 161–62
    and brochure, 141
    keeping simple, 117–18
    posting, 47, 117–18
    sample, 119
    See also Rules of operation

Illness, 163
Illustrations for brochure, 142
Income, 175–76
    estimating, 17–18
    and record keeping, 173
Incorporation, 175
Inn Times, The, magazine, 142
Insurance, 11, 126–27, 162, 175
    agent, 122–23, 126–27
    companies, 186–87
    rates, 123
    and taxes, 174
Ironing board, 48

Jacuzzi tub, 132

Keys
    house, 124
    and house rules, 116
    room, 48
King-sized beds, 42, 44
Kitchen, 30–32
    breakfast in, 96
    guests' access to, 115
Knickknacks, 54

Laundering, 44, 66
    costs, 11
Lawsuits, 35
Lawyer, 36
Liability, and incorporation, 175
Library, 82
Licenses and permits, 7, 162
Life's Little Instruction Book (Brown), 53
Lights
    bathroom, 68
    bedroom, 44
    closet, 46
    fixtures, 53
Living quarters, your own, 30, 77
Living room(s), 30–32, 77–82
    and business travelers, 86
    number of, 81–82
    well-appointed, 79–82
    See also Common or public rooms
Location, 23–25, 26, 37
Locks
    bathroom, 70
    bedroom, 48, 127
    and safety, 124
Loveseat, 49, 79
Luggage rack, 46

Magazine advertising, 137–38
Mailing list, 178–79
Mail order catalogues, 187–89
Maps and brochures of area, 164
Market, and rates, 132–33

Master bedroom, 151–52
 location, 30, 34
Mattresses, 11, 42, 52
Menus
 for breakfast, 100, 102–3
 from local restaurants, 164
Midweek rates, 134, 174
Minimum stay requirements, 133, 140
Mirror
 bathroom, 65–66
 bedroom, 46, 54
Muffins, 91, 93

Napkins, 98
Neighbors, 32–33
Newsletter, 178
Newspaper
 advertising, 138
 feature writers, 140

Off-limits areas, 114
Off-season
 packages, 178
 rates, 133
Orange Julius, 108
Orange Waffles, 106–7
Organization, and hospitality, 160–62
Outbuildings, 31–32
Outdoor areas, 82–86, 114
Overbooking
 avoiding, 145, 150
 what to do in case of, 150–52

Painting, 53, 67–68
Palmer's Chart House, 106
Pancakes, Pecan (Pancakes Supreme), 104–5
Pantry, 31
 stocking, 101, 108, 161
Paper towels, 62
Parking, 32–33, 115
Parmesan Potatoes, 107
Patios, 82, 83–84, 132

Payment
 forms of, 120–21
 handling, at check-in, 152–54
Pears Hersey, Baked, 108–9
Pecan Pancakes (Pancakes Supreme), 104–5
Personal activities, 13
Personal service, 9
Pets, rules about, 120
Piano, 80
Picnicking, 85–86
Pillowcases, 43, 45
Pillow covers, 45
Pillows, 43, 45
Pillow shams, 45, 53
Plants, 80, 83
Porch, 34, 82
Portable toilet, 52
Postcards, 49
Potatoes, Parmesan, 106–7
Privacy
 and common rooms, 77, 78–79
 and hospitality, 162
 and layout, 30–32, 37, 52
 loss of, 15
 and master bedroom, 30
 and outdoor areas, 84
Private bathroom, 52, 59
 cleaning, 63
 and rates, 132
Processing fee, 121
Profits, vs. expenses, 11, 17–18, 175–76
Property taxes, 174
Publicity, free, 140

Queen-sized beds, 42, 44
Questionnaire, 35
Quick breads, 108
Quitting your job, 17–18

Radios
 in bedrooms, 50
 in living room, 80

Rates, 17, 162
and bathroom, 59, 64, 72
and bed, 42
and competitiveness, 136
and credit cards, 135
and decorating, 53
and discounts, 134–35
how to figure, 131–36
listing, in brochure, 141
and record keeping, 174
seasonal and weekend, 133–34
quoting, when taking reservations, 148
and taxes, 136
and telephone, 51
Reading chairs, 49
Reading lamps, 49, 79
Reading materials, 49, 80
Receipt
for expenses, 173
for guest payment, 153–54
Recipes
Baked Eggs with Herbs and Cheese, 105
Baked Pears Hersey, 108–9
Buttermilk Biscuits, 104
Orange Julius, 107–8
Orange Waffles, 106–7
Parmesan Potatoes, 107
Pecan Pancakes (Pancakes Supreme), 104–5
Record keeping, 154, 173, 175
Refrigerator, 84–85, 115
Renovation and restoration, 25–26, 29, 32
costs, 18–19
and fire safety features, 123
and taxes, 174
Reservation(s), 35
calendar, 7, 140, 145, 150, 152
file, 150, 154
how to take, 143–52
services, 154–55, 183
sheets, 145–50, 152
system, 161
Restaurant recommendations, 164, 165

Retirement
plan, 15
running a B&B in, 15, 16
Roof, 32
Room tax, 136
Rugs, 176
bathroom, 69
bedroom, 47
Rules of operation, 118–22. *See also* House
rules

Safety, 122–26
and alcohol, drugs and allergic reactions,
124–26
bathroom, 124
fire, 122–23
and locks, 124
and valuables, 127
Screening guests, 144
Seasonal business, 23. *See also* Off-season
Secondhand shops, 53
Security system, 127
Self-employment taxes, 15
Semiprivate baths, 63–64
Senior citizen discount, 135
Septic system, 31, 36
Serving, 99
Shades or blinds, 19, 46, 52, 70
Sheets, 11, 43, 45
changing, 54
Sherry, 82, 125–26
Shower, 66–67
curtains or door, 67
mat, 124
Side tables, 79
Sign, 140
Sims, Louise, 107
Single rooms, 44
Sink, 65
Sitting room, 51. *See also* Suite
Skiers, 95, 138
Skylight, 64

Sleigh beds, 42

Smoke detectors, 19, 47, 123

Smoking rules, 86, 113–14

Soap, 70

Sofa, 49

Sound insulation, 29, 32

Specialty locations, 25

Spin-off business, 176–77

Sport fishermen, 95

Sprinkler system, 123

Stairs, 30–32, 34
    and fire safety, 123

Stamps, 11

Start-up costs, 18–19, 32, 175–76

Stationery, 11, 143

Stenciling, 53, 54

Style, 52–54, 80–81. *See also* Furnishing
    and decor

Sugar substitutes, 102

"Suggestion" box, 177–78

Suites, 29, 51

Sun room, 82

Swimming pool, 84

Switchplates, 54

Table, 49
    setting, 98

Tablecloth, 98

Tax(es)
    advantages, 16–17, 25, 174
    and rates, 136

Tea
    afternoon, 6, 82, 132, 160
    breakfast, 95
    herb, 102

Teaching, 16

Telephone
    in bedrooms, 50–51, 86
    expenses, 11
    lines, 144–45
    in living room, 79–80
    rules, 115
    yellow pages advertising, 139

Television
    in bedrooms, 50, 86
    in living room, 79, 81
    and rates, 132

Tennis courts, 84

Tile, 65, 66–67

Time, 11, 13. *See also* Arrival time; Break-
    fast time; Check-in time

Tissue, 11, 48, 69

Toilet, 66

Toilet paper, 11, 63, 66

Tourism departments, 136–37, 164

Towel bars, 68–69

Towels, 11, 54, 61
    importance of, 71
    and shared bathroom, 62–63

Towel valets, 48, 61, 62, 63

Trade publications, 182–83

Trunk, 46

Tub, 66–67
    claw-foot, 67
    mat, 124

"Turn-key" operation, 35

Twin-sized beds, 42, 44

Utility bills, 174

Vacations, taking your own, 163

Vacation travelers, 24–25

Vacuuming, 54, 55

Valuables, protecting your own, 127

Vegetarians, 102

Ventilation, 64, 65

Views, 132

Waffles, Orange, 106

Wallpaper, 53, 68

Walls and ceilings, 67–68

Wastebasket, 48, 54, 63, 69

Water pressure, 32, 67

Weather, 35–36, 153

Wedding parties, 84

Weekend rates, 133–34, 174
Window
  bathroom, 64, 65, 70
  bedroom, 46
  condition of, 32
  living room, 80–81
  See also Drapes and curtains; Shades or blinds
Wine, 125–26

Working at home, 9–10, 14–15
Writing table, 49–50, 79

Yankee magazine, 137–38
Yard, 26, 33–34, 84–85, 114
Yard sales, 53
Year-round business, 23–25, 35–36

Zoning, 27–28, 37, 92